Scenarios and Information Design

CHANDOS
INFORMATION PROFESSIONAL SERIES

Series Editor: Ruth Rikowski
(email: Rikowskigr@aol.com)

Chandos' new series of books are aimed at the busy information professional. They have been specially commissioned to provide the reader with an authoritative view of current thinking. They are designed to provide easy-to-read and (most importantly) practical coverage of topics that are of interest to librarians and other information professionals. If you would like a full listing of current and forthcoming titles, please visit our web site **www.chandospublishing.com** or contact Hannah Grace-Williams on email info@chandospublishing.com or telephone number +44 (0) 1865 884447.

New authors: we are always pleased to receive ideas for new titles; if you would like to write a book for Chandos, please contact Dr Glyn Jones on email gjones@chandospublishing.com or telephone number +44 (0) 1865 884447.

Bulk orders: some organisations buy a number of copies of our books. If you are interested in doing this, we would be pleased to discuss a discount. Please contact Hannah Grace-Williams on email info@chandospublishing.com or telephone number +44 (0) 1865 884447.

Scenarios and Information Design

A user-oriented practical guide

MARY LYNN RICE-LIVELY
AND
HSIN-LIANG CHEN

Chandos Publishing
Oxford • England

Chandos Publishing (Oxford) Limited
Chandos House
5 & 6 Steadys Lane
Stanton Harcourt
Oxford OX29 5RL
UK
Tel: +44 (0) 1865 884447 Fax: +44 (0) 1865 884448
Email: info@chandospublishing.com
www.chandospublishing.com

First published in Great Britain in 2006

ISBN:
1 84334 061 5 (paperback)
1 84334 062 3 (hardback)

© Mary Lynn Rice-Lively and Hsin-Liang Chen, 2006

British Library Cataloguing-in-Publication Data.
A catalogue record for this book is available from the British Library.

Typeset by Domex e-Data Pvt. Ltd.
Printed in the UK and USA.

Contents

List of figures and tables

Figures

Tables

About the authors

Mary Lynn Rice-Lively is the Associate Dean at the University of Texas at Austin's School of Information. She worked in library and information services for over 15 years before returning to take a PhD in information studies. In Dallas, Texas she held management positions at the Dallas Public Library and the City of Dallas Mayor and Council Office. After moving to Austin, Texas in 1988 she worked in management positions at the University of Texas' Tarlton Law Library and in the University Libraries. She has taught in the School of Information since 1993 and has facilitated dozens of Internet and technology workshops throughout the United States and abroad. Her research and publishing interests include the culture of networked communities, learning and information technologies, social sense-making, and qualitative research in networked environments. Her degrees include a PhD and BA from UT-Austin, and an MLS from the University of North Texas.

The author may be contacted as follows:

Mary Lynn Rice-Lively
Associate Dean
School of Information
The University of Texas at Austin
E-mail: *marylynn@ischool.utexas.edu*

Hsin-Liang (Oliver) Chen is an assistant professor in the School of Information at the University of Texas at Austin where he teaches and conducts research in the areas of instructional technology, multimedia design, image retrieval, user studies, human–computer interaction and information system evaluation. He has published numerous papers on digital museums, digital libraries for K-12 education and digital video libraries for college students. Dr Chen received his Bachelor's degree in Library Science from Fu-Jen Catholic University in Taiwan (1992), his Masters degree in Educational Communication and Technology from New York University (1995) and his PhD in Library and Information Science from the University of Pittsburgh (1999).

The author may be contacted as follows:

Hsin-Liang Chen
Assistant Professor
School of Information
The University of Texas at Austin
E-mail: *chen@ischool.utexas.edu*

Introduction and overview

Why do we need scenarios for information system design?

As human consumers of information we regularly encounter information and interact with a variety of physical and electronic information systems. For example, recall the last time you walked around a neighborhood where you had never been before. First, you would have had to locate directional signs, then, hopefully, you would have been able to decipher the signs to know where you were, make decisions about which direction to take next and, ultimately, solve the problem of how to locate your destination. Or what happened the last time you were driving in an unfamiliar city where you had to both navigate traffic at 60 mph and watch out for crucial directional signs to guide you to the proper exit to your destination. Each different 'information bearing system' encountered during a walk around an unfamiliar neighborhood or drive on a confusing freeway illustrates the complexity of our physical information environment. As we continue our rapid journey into the digital era, we repeatedly encounter similar situations in a digital (or, if you prefer, a networked) environment. Have you booked an airline reservation online? How long did it take you to successfully complete the form(s)? Did you succeed? Did you have to change to a compatible web browser because your favorite browser would not work with the reservation system? If your initial efforts to complete this or a similar task were successful, congratulations! If not, how long did it take you to maneuver around the quirks of the system, and how did you respond during this experience? Challenges such as these persist in our daily lives in both the physical and electronic worlds. As information users, we are called upon to interact with information and information systems in a variety of environments and our actions rely on feedback from those information systems. Because interaction between people and information systems is very individualized and complicated, the use of scenarios can provide information designers with new ways to better understand and plan for such interactions.

The above examples demonstrate that information design must accommodate the needs of users as well as their interactions with information and information systems. Information designers can use scenarios to capture target users' characteristics and actions while designing an information system. As we explore later in this book, there is a wide range of professionals who participate in the information system design process. (The authors use the term information systems broadly throughout this book.) Such systems might be designed for marketing strategists to study potential demands, computer engineers to write codes, graphic designers to create layouts, etc. Information design requires teamwork, and each team member must use his or her talent to understand users and their environments or the particular context in which they will use the information system.

For instance, marketing strategists must study who lives in a particular neighbourhood and who makes frequent visits to that neighborhood as well as the purpose of those visits. Graphic designers must know what colors, fonts, and formats should be utilized for the guiding information and make decisions about the placement of such information, while computer engineers create devices or hardware to implement the graphic designers' plans. Each team member contributes important knowledge to collect different pieces of data from target users. From this data the entire design team can construct a scenario that more accurately illustrates the targeted users and the environment. In the next section we will discuss the definition, purpose and use of scenarios in information design projects.

What are scenarios?

Scenarios are stories (Carroll, 2000). For this reason information designers must be good storytellers. A good storyteller becomes acquainted with the audience and works to engage them in the storytelling. Through interaction with the audience-participants the storyteller creates stories that evolve with the feedback from that audience. As good storytellers, information designers are able to envision their design by imagining how the targeted audience will use the system under development.

Scenarios guide information designers in planning the information system. Through a thoughtfully developed scenario, the designer can:

- begin the design plan;
- define the necessary project steps;
- establish the process workflows;
- identify the targeted users;
- distinguish between system users' activities;
- institute communication channels with users and the design team; and
- implement a useful, reliable system.

To construct a story an information designer begins by identifying the actor (user) and his or her acting sequences. In most cases, scenarios involve multiple actors interlinking in highly complicated acting sequences. The information designer must also select the environments (or context) within which those actors act and react to each other, as exemplified in the description above of finding your way in a new neighborhood. Consider, for example, the scenario in Figure 1.1.

Most of us have had similar experiences when we are seeking information or directional cues from our environment to find our way to a particular destination. The information designer must attempt to recreate the context for a user of a particular information system. Through the construction of a story (or scenario) information designers can envision

Figure 1.1   Wayfinding scenario

The setting is a neighborhood in a big metropolitan city. You, a female recently graduated from a small liberal college located in a small Midwestern town, are dragging a huge suitcase and walking alone on the street while you try to locate your aunt's townhouse. 'It should be here, 236 Green Street,' you comment to yourself. You have followed the directions in your aunt's letter and have circled the same blocks several times. Unfortunately, some street signs are out and some houses do not have their numbers on the doors. It is obvious that you must ask people for directions.

You ask someone passing, 'Excuse me, do you know where Green Street is?'

The person replies, 'Sorry, I don't live in this area.'

The next person you see, you ask, 'Excuse me, could you direct me to Green Street?' The person hurries off saying, 'Oh, I have to catch the bus, sorry.'

how the actor(s) act, react and interact with each other and with available information in a particular environment(s) initially, and then how they act after the implementation of an information system. With this example we aim to have convinced you of the importance of taking a scenario-based approach to information design projects. If you still not convinced, then continue reading!

Scenario-less planning: what can go wrong?

In 2000, Columbia University established Fathom.com, a for-profit distance education website. This online-learning venture was partnered with the American Film Institute, the British Library, Cambridge University Press, the London School of Economics and Political Science, the Natural History Museum in London, the New York Public Library, RAND, the Science Museum in London, the University of Chicago, the University of Michigan system, the Victorian & Albert Museum and the Woods Hole Oceanographic Institution. Unfortunately, in 2003, after spending $25 million dollars, Columbia University ended the Fathom.com venture as it could not provide support to its users to overcome the difficulties with the system. Ann Kirschner, the company's chief executive, said: 'One of the greatest barriers to online learning was people's unfamiliarity with the process ... They know what a book is. They know what a course is. But what exactly is an online course? That they didn't know' (Arenson, 2003). Other universities such as New York University, Temple University, and the University of Maryland University College have already closed their online programs.

These examples provide expensive lessons from the dot.com era, when people thought that the Internet could provide endless opportunities. The Internet may well offer many opportunities for education, work, commerce, and communication. Nonetheless, before attaining success, information designers must answer the question of how people will use and adopt an Internet-based service in their daily life and work. Information designers should go beyond systems implementation to consider their users and to know their 'stories.' A thorough understanding of the target users of the system should guide every step of the information systems design process, the goal being to provide the users with easy access to information.

Digital information design demands that designers both cultivate an open perspective and develop new skills to create information spaces that have imaginative and varied uses by diverse constituencies. The design of effective websites, software interfaces and other digital media demand an understanding not only of design principles and a range of markup language expertise, but also a bit of psychology, ethnography, and cognitive science. This book aims to guide the reader to a broad but practical understanding of the theoretical foundations of scenario construction and user-focused information design. Case studies drawn from the real world will reinforce the practical guidelines outlined in each chapter. Additionally, at the conclusion of each chapter, practical exercises will facilitate the application of the concepts explored, as the reader develops a strategic understanding of user-oriented information design techniques and scenario planning.

The structure of the book

Part 1 of this book, Practical Theories, includes three chapters (Chapters 2–4) that build the theoretical foundation to understand user-oriented scenario-based information design through a concise and practical exploration of the theories. In Chapter 2, 'Framework and fundamentals,' the authors construct the framework for this practical guide to scenario design. Among the topics included are a discussion of the tools and techniques used to identify user groups when beginning an information system design project. The exploration includes the methods used to determine the organizational and social complexities of understanding an individual or group of information users, including developing the long- and short-term goals for the system, and budgetary and time constraints. Examples and analysis of real-world examples reinforce this discussion.

Chapter 3 entitled 'Organizational cultures: ecological and cognitive approaches' considers how the information design process works to include the perspectives of individuals and organizations. Among the techniques are the inclusion of an open systems view of organizations using ethnographic research methodologies to explain the culture of an organization and how individuals work and interact within that system. How does organizational behaviour change when external vendors or consultants are involved in the information design process? The client and the consultant must be attuned to the different 'ways of knowing': a vendor with product to sell that is guaranteed to fit the needs of a client and a client with a specific service or operational need. Readers will explore how to utilize the predictable collision of values and 'needs' (prospective income versus desired product) as a creative and constructive force. Examples from industry substantiate how the two types of unreality – what the vendor says they can do and what the client wants – can either condemn a project or produce a compromise with both sides satisfied.

Chapter 4, 'Communicating with stakeholders,' explores who should be involved in the planning of an information system. What methods of communication will be used to keep participants and planners informed? How will participants and developers stay on track with plans and concepts? How will progress be tracked and deadlines adapted to the realities of the project?

Part 2 of the book, Theoretical Practices, guides the reader into an exploration of the fundamental theories that 'inform' information design projects. In Chapter 5, 'Managing scenario design projects and knowledge,' we consider the critical need for knowledge management in information design projects. A review of the scholarly literature reveals a wide range of definitions of knowledge management. For the purposes of this book we use knowledge management as 'a problem of capturing, organizing, and retrieving information, ... an activity that is inextricably bound up with human cognition and in a human context' (Thomas, Kellogg and Erickson, 2001: 863). Information design is not a linear sequential activity. It requires multitasking and parallel processing of tasks such as planning and project management. Basic project management principles will be identified and how they can be employed in knowledge management. The chapter will also provide guidelines on how to determine and monitor short- and long-term goals for communication and management of information/knowledge.

Chapter 6, 'Presentation of ideas,' outlines a formula to guide the information designer on how to establish a workable timeline. Questions are explored, such as how to determine media delivery platform(s) and media format(s) and what is involved in estimating the need for human and other resources and costs. How are ideas born during the project, archived and preserved but perhaps not employed?

The chapter also provides guidelines for employing both an external and internal view of the project. Are there elements of the project that should be outsourced? In what ways can project team members maintain an unfettered non-institutionalized perspective. The authors offer examples of how to establish the lifecycle timeline and people in charge. Should the project team use a computer-based content management system to monitor the cycle? What are the best ways to record and analyze follow-up discussions? Are there measures in place to protect and limit access to property or intellectual content of the information system during development?

The 'life cycle' of ideas is explored in Chapter 7. Team members in the design process agree that ideas evolve during the development of an information system project. In the beginning of the project, stakeholders contribute their ideas by using different media. At some point in the project some ideas are implemented while others are set aside for reconsideration. In such a dynamic and fast-paced development, we need to understand how to manage, make use of and archive this intellectual capital. Among the concepts explored in this chapter are the management of knowledge, documents and assets.

In Chapter 8, 'Documentation and prototyping,' models and examples guide information designers in setting standards for the information system prototype. How do the standards fit into project management? What are the plans for the use and testing of prototypes? How will client testing be done and what measures will be taken to align the client's 'dream' with reality?

The book's final chapter summarizes topics regarding project completion, plans for project evaluation and system evaluation.

References

Arenson, K.W. (2003) 'Columbia's Internet concern will soon go out of business,' *New York Times*, January 7.

Carroll, J.M. (2000) *Making Use: Scenario-Based Design of Human–Computer Interactions*. Cambridge, MA: MIT Press.

Thomas, J.C., Kellogg, W.A., and Erickson, T. (2001) 'The knowledge management puzzle: human and social factors in knowledge management,' *IBM Systems Journal*, 40 (4): 863–84.

Part 1
Practical Theories

2

Framework and fundamentals

Purpose of the system and formation of the design team

When beginning an information system design, the first question to ask is, 'Who is going to use the system?' While the question appears to be a simple one, it often challenges information designers. 'We know there are potential users, but we really do not know how to identify them!' This is especially true when the user potentially is anyone with access to the Web. Even though the task sounds daunting, information designers must identify the primary user group(s) for the proposed system, because identifying the primary user group(s) guides the information designers as they build the foundation of the information system. In a sentence, *it establishes the goals for the system.*

Let's consider the design of an internal information system such as an organization's intranet. The design team must begin with analyzing the entire organization from both vertical and horizontal perspectives. The team also examines interdepartmental relationships for information sharing and exchange. Be prepared, as the analysis can be complicated and problematic. Why? Politics and people!

First, the purpose of the system must be determined. Designers must ask questions such as, 'Will it be an internal system or open to users external to the organization, or will it be a combination of both?' 'Who has responsibility for the design and implementation?' 'Will these tasks be the responsibility of the information technology department or an outside consulting firm?' The answers to these questions are fundamental to the identification of the primary user group(s). To plan an internal system all employees and their work tasks must be studied and represented in the system design. For an external system, a target user/customer group(s) should be studied. The design team must track the flow and exchange of information when internal and external systems are combined. Consider, for example, the user of a customer services system. When a customer service agent receives a question from a customer about a monthly bill, the agent should be able to see the same layout of the customer's monthly bill to facilitate an efficient and intelligent response to the customer's questions. Or the agent should be able to forward the customer's phone call and question to another agent with previously gathered information accompanying the transfer. To illustrate a frustrating exchange we've probably all experienced consider that shown in Figure 2.1. You are talking to the second customer services agent with regard to your monthly phone bill. Whether accidentally or not, your call is disconnected before you resolve your query. Probably by this stage, you would be an angry customer!

The dialogue in Figure 2.1 recreates a scenario common to many of us. Poorly designed systems not only frustrate customers and service agents, but they can also drive customers away and damage a company's business. A well-planned and integrated information system that anticipates how to avoid such situations should be the goal of every design team.

Once the design team has identified the primary user group(s) they must proceed with the purpose of the information system. While it may seem basic, clearly

Figure 2.1 A phone conversation between a customer and a service agent

'Excuse me, sir, but I have already explained my situation to the first customer services agent. My question is, why was I charged $150.00 last month?'

'Mr Smith, I'm sorry to have to ask you to explain your situation again. I can't see that record. Can you tell me to whom you spoke last time? Maybe I can contact them?'

'I don't remember his name. OK, let me explain it to you again. According to my bill, there was a charge of $150.00 on 15 July. I do not know why. I've not purchased anything on this account in six months.'

'Mr Smith, sorry, but I can't see the bill on my computer.'

'What?'

'Yes, please call the accounting department.'

'Can't you forward my call to the accounting department?'

defining the purpose of the system at the beginning of the design process is crucial to project success. Unfortunately, there are many real-life cases that illustrate that ignorance of or ambiguity in the system's core purpose often demands extra development time, as well as costs more money and personnel than budgeted to complete the system. Consider the example provided in Figure 2.2.

The PeopleSoft and IU example demonstrates why the design team must identify who is undertaking the design responsibility. As we see, according to Don Hossler, 'Almost nobody can afford to program all of the customizations overnight.' Nonetheless, contracting with an outside consulting firm to design an information system adds yet another layer of complexity to the design and completion of the system. Why? Because it is more difficult for an outside design team to gain access to in-depth information

Figure 2.2 PeopleSoft vs. Indiana University at Bloomington (Olsen, 2002)

In December 2002, the faculty council at Indiana University (IU) at Bloomington decided to end the *GardPact* program, a popular four-years-and-out graduation policy, because the university had to pay an initial charge of $230,000 and an annual maintenance expense of $60,000 to its PeopleSoft student records system to accommodate the policy (Olsen, 2002). According to Don Hossler, Associate President for Enrollments Services, 'Almost nobody can afford to program all of the customizations overnight.'

about the organization and to establish critical channels of communication. We will discuss strategies for addressing these concerns in more detail in Chapters 3 and 4.

Meanwhile, system designers must acknowledge the complicated working relationships among different entities. Figure 2.3 illustrates this point.

Figure 2.3 presents the relationships between the *information system* (internal and external) and the *design team* (external and internal). Client organization employees use an internal information system for security and business reasons, while an external system can serve as an information kiosk for customers to learn about the organization's latest news and merchandising. The internal design team is comprised of organization employees from one or several departments and an external design team which may be drawn from an outside consulting firm.

After the design team determines the purpose of the system, it is much easier to identify the primary user group(s). An organization-wide accounting system for traveling, for instance, is undergoing a redesign to streamline the process. Each employee is required to submit his or her travel request

Figure 2.3 Four relationships among information systems and design teams

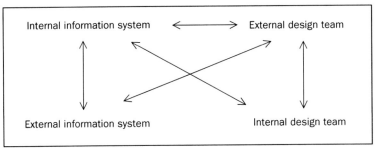

online first to be approved by the boss, department head and the accounting department. The assignment to finish the project goes to the IT department. Since it is a case of an internal system vs. an internal design team, the IT department can obtain current application forms from the accounting department, observe employees filling out the forms, and so on. If the administration wants to eliminate some redundant steps, then the IT department should talk to some top-level administrators. By now, you should understand what we have meant by 'politics'! To carry out the system design, the design team has to knock on the door of its client users to gather design details. Yes, it is all about politics. Remember, in this example we are talking about the case of an internal system vs. an internal design team only.

An external system requires the internal design team to spend more time and energy in understanding the target customers. If the organization decides to outsource the project, then it must be decided which department should document all the details about the internal users and external users and develop a blueprint for system requirements, which department is responsible for approving the requirements and overseeing and monitoring the evolution of the project during the design process, and which department will be responsible for approving the requirements and overseeing and monitoring the evolution of the project during the design process. A purposeful chain of events must take place to begin the information design process. First, the purpose of the system must be determined at the beginning of the design process. Second, the purpose of the system and the formation of the design team determines the complexity of the communications. Third, the workflow and responsibilities must be clearly identified and assigned.

The design planning process is already getting very complicated, and we have yet to discuss the target user group! Nevertheless, it is very important to outline the duties of the design team before identifying the user group.

Identify user groups

The next step is to focus on the user group and the environment in which the system will be used. Once the purpose of the system has been decided, the design team should have a better idea about how to investigate the target user group and its environments. Take, for example, an organization that wants its employees to report their weekly assignments online. In this example all the employees in the organization comprise the user group. Should the design team talk to every employee? What should they do if the organization has more than 1,000 employees and they are in several cities or states? Clearly, interviewing all 1,000 employees is not practical. Are you thinking of sampling? Excellent! This strategy is a good way to move the project forward. What is the planned procedure to sample the target users? The design team needs information on the employees in each location from the Human Resources office. The information should report each employee's job duties, office environment, work shifts, and other relevant aspects of their workflow. All of this information assists the design team to select data sets for inclusion in the information system design.

What about your customers? Do customers need to be included in the system? Many marketing consulting firms collect and sell to client companies information on customer shopping behaviors. By now most of us know why stores ask us to complete forms when you shop there. Such forms are one of several ways for stores to collect unique customer information and interests. When do you shop? How often do you make purchases? What do you buy, and for whom are you shopping? What are your hobbies? Your shopping behaviors are the foundation of their marketing strategies. When designing a customer system, the design team must collect such information from the marketing department or the customer services department to shape the look, feel and use of the system under design.

After obtaining and analyzing the users' information, the design team can sample the users based on relevant selection criteria. Several categories should be considered: gender, age, geographic location, language, education, cultural and ethnic background, department/unit, job position, etc. The value of these categories may vary from system to system depending upon the purpose of the system. Think back to our weekly work-time report example. If the design team studies employees in only one location, it is very likely to collect biased information. For example, the data collected from white-collar workers in an office building in a big city may be very different from the data collected from factory technicians in a suburban area.

Sometimes the selection of the target user group can take another direction. For example, suppose an organization wants to attract a new group of customers and a new information system is planned for the users. Therefore the purpose of the new information system is predetermined.

When identifying user groups, one important issue must be kept in mind at all times: users are actors in a scenario/scenarios and the design team wants to observe those actors' actions in a meaningful context or environment. Therefore who is going to observe the users, where the users will be observed, how the users will be observed, what to observe, how to present the observations and how to integrate the data collected from the observations into the system design are important steps in the entire process. Specific strategies for better understanding your users are discussed in Chapter 3.

Identify user groups' environments

Let's consider one of the many examples of marketing strategies gathered from our day-to-day physical environment. For example, have you ever been bothered by supermarkets and stores in your neighborhood when they re-shelf the merchandise supposedly to satisfy customers' shopping behaviors and to entice customers to buy more or to select something not on their shopping list? On the other hand, when merchandise is rearranged in this way the store may be annoying its customers who now have to spend more time finding items on their shopping list since they are no longer found in familiar locations.

Another example concerns directional signs in buildings and on highways. Often the placement and design of such signs do more to confuse us and than deliver anticipated or required information. Often remedial signs must be added to improve the conditions of ill-designed buildings and highways. Have you ever gone round in circles at the airport in an attempt to find your flight departure gate? Have you missed your flight after reading confusing or ill-placed signs? Or after a long, circuitous walk to find a restroom, have you suddenly found a better route? These examples from the physical environment are not only annoying and frustrating but can be dangerous. And it doesn't take too much imagination to conjure up similar problems in the networked environment.

On the Web, we all have witnessed many e-commerce sites that are constantly changing their layout and structure. An organization may want to consider the frequency of a customer system update. Even though these business establishments try to improve their services through redesign efforts, are they aware that they may instead have confused their customers and lost business? Users also encounter similar difficulties when using a new version of software. Software companies tend to launch a new version of software in a fast-paced environment that spends little or no time on user testing. Newly added functions (some necessary and some not) and re-grouped functions within software programs often frustrate users as well as adding unanticipated costs to purchasing budgets.

So that you may avoid the pitfalls that these unnamed software companies and website designers have fallen into, the following section of this chapter introduces several data collection techniques that will provide the design team with critical insight into their potential system users.

Methods for identifying users and their environments

User survey

Questionnaires are widely used for data collection. A well-designed questionnaire aims to collect valid and reliable data;

however, the types of questions, the arrangement of questions/choices, the distribution/recall of the questionnaires and the interpretation of the data can dramatically affect the validation and reliability of the questionnaire. To avoid these errors, the design team must craft questionnaires which are grounded in the goals of the system and derive questions from each goal. Why is a particular question asked? What data can the design team obtain by asking a particular question? If it is a multiple-choice question, does the team provide sufficient choices to the respondent? In the meantime, the design also needs to integrate specific strategies for data coding and interpretation into the questionnaire format, as in, for example, Figure 2.4.

In this case, a company wants to know the current utilization of e-mail among its employees. The design team can not only obtain descriptive data of gender and use from questions 1 and 2, but they can also analyze the relationship between gender and e-mail use. The data show that 56 female and 48 male employees answered the survey. Thirty-five of the 104 employees checked e-mail massages once a

Figure 2.4 **Example of questionnaire format**

Question 1: Gender: __ Female __ Male

Question 2: How often per day do you check e-mail messages at work?
                    __ Once __ 2–4 times __ 5–6 times __ 7–8 times

Data:

Question 1: Gender: <u>56</u> Female <u>48</u> Male

Question 2: How often per day do you check e-mail messages at work?
                    <u>35</u> Once <u>26</u> 2–4 times <u>33</u> 5–6 times <u>10</u> 7–8 times

day, 26 did 2–4 times, 33 5–6 times, and 10 7–8 times. The descriptive data presents a simple picture of the employees' e-mail usage. It does not, however, provide the design team any further information such as whether female or male employees check e-mail messages more often or not. Nonetheless, the team can run a correlation analysis between questions 1 and 2 to discover which gender of employees checks e-mail messages more often. This approach will help the team achieve a more in-depth and comprehensive data analysis.

The team must also know how to sample and collect the questionnaires. In the above example, 58 female and 46 male employees were surveyed. Perhaps this company has 58 female and 46 male employees. Is it ethical for the design team to use the data as representative of employees' opinions? If they were samples from the company, then the data can be biased because the number of female respondents is slightly higher than the number of male respondents. Therefore the design team needs to realign the numbers of the two sub-groups.

Take care when selecting a particular order for the questions. The design team must arrange the questions in an order that doesn't bias or direct responses. Include critical information with particular questions, unless such recall is part of the questionnaire design. For example, suppose the design team wants to know the user's reaction to a new system interface. Snapshots of the interface should be presented with questions because respondents may not be able to recall the details of the interface and so provide the wrong feedback.

Other research methods such as focus groups and interviews should be used to complement the use of the questionnaire. Often respondents do not complete all of the questions in a questionnaire or provide vague answers. If the design team administers both a questionnaire and interviews, the team should use numbers to link a respondent to their questionnaire. During the interviews, the team can ask the respondents to clarify their answers or request a more detailed reply. Through the use of this combined technique the team can collect more complete and rich information. However, the procedure should be carried out in a consistent manner and comply with the questionnaire design.

The design team can also create websites with online questionnaires designed for convenient data coding and analysis. Many websites provide services for customized questionnaires and data analysis (Figure 2.5). More complex, database-driven websites can generate basic graphics, such as pie or bar charts, from the answers provided for each question. Again, the team should go beyond using just the simple descriptive data and analyze the data from several related questions. To do this, the team needs to know how to code data, input the data into statistical programs and run the appropriate statistical analyses. When such data analysis is considered beforehand, the design team can monitor the smooth collection of data and harvest data that will provide valuable direction to the design project.

After identifying the target user group, the design teams must survey all existing systems and their functionalities from the very beginning of the project. This is very difficult task, but it must be done. The more comprehensive the survey the more prepared the design team will be to avoid pitfalls. In many ways the exercise is like planning a party at home. First, you must know who is coming to the party (*identify target users*). If it is a formal party, the host might request that the guests specify their dietary and drink preferences. After the guests arrive at your place, you ask

Figure 2.5 Samples of online questionnaires

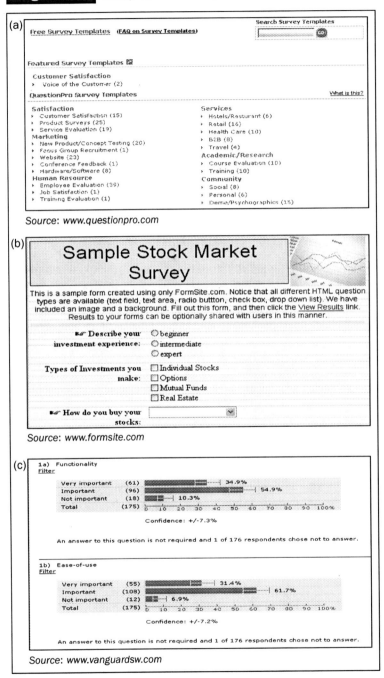

Source: www.questionpro.com

Source: www.formsite.com

Source: www.vanguardsw.com

everyone what he or she would like to drink and you have the drinks and snacks already prepared in the kitchen.

Another scenario that illustrates our human need for efficiency of action follows. You are watching TV with friends. During the commercials, you want to grab a drink from the refrigerator. Before you go into the kitchen you ask everyone in the room what they want to drink because you want to accomplish the task with only *one* trip to the kitchen.

Other considerations for identifying users and their environments

A comprehensive survey guides the design team in collecting input from all the offices involved in the process. The survey also assists the design team in developing their blueprint for the project. In the blueprint the design team clearly describes the long-term and short-term goals based on their understanding of how many components and sub-systems the project will entail. The team lays out the priorities for implementation, deadlines, costs, etc.

A blueprint for the project is even more important when an outside consulting firm is involved. The blueprint will become part of the contract between the organization (client) and the consulting firm (contractor). Legal and financial responsibilities are clearly identified in the contract for both parties.

In the blueprint, long-term and short-term goals are identified by the input from all organizational units. Several important factors for inclusion in this stage are each unit's:

- functions
- budget

- personnel
- time
- data sources.

These elements help the design team to establish priorities for the project. Let's return to the weekly report example. In this case, the design team needs to determine which area office will be the location for system implementation. The team may want to select the largest area office as the test location because it will offer a wider variety of possible situations for the system. On the other hand, if the team selects a smaller office as the test location it must acknowledge the fact that some uses or processes may not be available to test the system implementation fully. If the design team chooses several offices as test locations, hopefully the organization can afford to have multiple teams at the test sites to implement the system. The cost of multiple-unit testing and the personnel needed to implement such a project are the two additional factors that should be considered. If time allows, the design team can travel to different sites. A final project decision relates to the selection of the data sources that will populate the system. Data sources often are difficult to identify. Consider the following example: a library plans to develop a digital image system for an important collection of photographs. Are the images physical or digital files? Who owns the intellectual property rights to the collection? If they are to be scanned, are they already catalogued or classified in some other system? Is quality scanning equipment available for the project? What are the other steps involved in preparing the collection for an online system?

After determining the long-term and short-term goals, the design team should be able to identify the variables that are important to implement the system. These variables may include individuals, sub-groups, the entire organization or multiple organizations. So far, we have considered the importance and complexity of identifying user groups. In the meantime, it is also important to consider the following characteristics of these components of the user group before moving a project forward:

1. *Individuals* – who can accelerate or slow down the development of the project. In an organization, we often come across so-called 'visionary' people who also hold important positions in the organization. If the vision of these people matches the goal of the project, the design team should meet them and enlist their support. On the other hand, the design team may face resistance to project goals from some influential members of the organization. Finding ways to minimize resistance is another challenge for the design team.

2. *Sub-groups* – which can be a special-interest group(s) from different offices in an organization. The special-interest group(s) may have studied the project for a long time and the design team should consult the group to obtain its members' experience. Some members of the special-interest group may serve on different committees to assist the design team on the development of the project.

3. *The entire organization* – the organizational culture and subcultures are important considerations in the development of the project. Employees' attitudes should be taken into account in the design of the new information system. New changes or requirements may cause unnecessary panic among employees and lead to possible failure of the project implementation. The design team must establish appropriate communication channels throughout the whole organization and the channels

should offer timely information about the project. We will discuss more details on this matter in Chapter 4.

4. *Multiple organizations (consortium)* – it is likely that several organizations may be involved in one information system. In this case the design team must consider the nature of the multiple organizations: their organizational cultures, missions, interests, etc. Several organizations may rush into a partnership without understanding possible conflict. We have seen this kind of problem in the business field such as in the Time Warner and America On Line merger. When companies merge or form a partnership, employees in different companies have to face new work procedures, new administrative requirements, new office 'languages,' etc. The design team must cope with these factors throughout the development of the project.

Once organizational components have been clarified for the project team, a final consideration for planning the project is whether a training program will be needed to ease organizational members into the adoption and use of the new system.

New human activities: training and education

Will the client organization embrace or reject the new information system? To some extent this depends upon how well designed the system is and the role that users played in the system development. Even the most elegantly designed system will necessitate education and training for both the design team and users. Training is expensive and time-consuming, with results that are difficult to measure. In many cases some organizations often ignore or are unwilling to spend time and expense on the need for education and training.

When the design team has thoroughly identified the user group(s), it is more likely the information system will serve the users well and require minimal training. Nonetheless, the design team must plan for the possible dilemma of how to accommodate unanticipated existing tasks within the new system. If the new information system requires new work procedures, the users must have a variety of mechanisms to learn these new procedures. To accommodate diverse learning styles, the design team should provide both a printed and an online user's manual, as well as service hotlines or chat forums for users to consult!

The design team must always seriously examine the existing users' practices. If the project budget and time are limited, the team must find a balance between users' existing practices, training, and the system's functionality. For a small group of system operators, a comprehensive new design may be possible. On the other hand, a large organization-wide system may not be implemented without comprehensive employee training over a prolonged period of time.

Organizations must have policies for the long-term and short-term goals of their information systems. These policies determine how often and to what extent the systems should be examined. Such policies also determine what data techniques and tools should be used to achieve the goals. Chapter 3 will explore in more depth alternative data-gathering techniques and tools to be used as appropriate by the design team. We will discuss these techniques and tools from ecological and cognitive approaches that emphasize the operations of the organization and its stakeholders.

Summary

Information designers must identify the primary user group(s) for the proposed system to establish the goals for the system. The goals should be examined in terms of organizational policies from long- and short-term perspectives. Once the primary user group(s) is identified, the design team can choose appropriate research methods to study the group(s). During the entire process of identifying and studying the user group(s), the design team must pay attention to time, budget, personnel, and other support resources to successfully finish the investigation.

Reference

Olsen, F. (2002) 'Software-coding costs force Indiana U. at Bloomington to drop a popular graduation guarantee,' *Chronicle of Higher Education*. Available at: *http://chronicle.com/free/2002/12/2002120501t.htm*.

3

Organizational cultures: ecological and cognitive approaches

Information systems of all types are designed for human use. Because humans are members of social groups and organizations, information designers must seek to involve users in the design of the information product and to envision human use of the product being designed. The organization for which an information product is being designed must to some extent be part of the design team (Erickson, 1995). To do so requires gaining some understanding of the systems (human and organizational) in which individuals live and work. This chapter will explore the nature of organizations and organizational cultures. We will also propose additional data-gathering techniques to contribute to the design team's understanding of organizations from both a macro- and a micro-level view. Let us begin with a macro view of the client organization by briefly exploring the theoretical definitions of organizations and a few simple strategies to better understand them.

Organizations defined

For the purposes of this discussion we define organizations as complex, dynamic social structures that exist to 'get work done.' Volumes have been written exploring a wide range of organizational theories. Design teams must seek to understand the client organization and the people who work there as a critical preparatory step to designing an information product or space for use by that organization.

Organizations exist to make ordinary human beings perform better than they seem capable of, to bring out whatever strengths there are in its members, and to use its power to help all the other members carry out their duties, as well as to produce or manage a product or provide a service. Peter F. Drucker, however, reminds us that:

> By now, however, it should have become clear that there is no such thing as the one right organization ... [Organizations are] a tool for making people productive in working together. As such, a given organization structure fits certain tasks in certain conditions and at certain times. (Drucker, 2001: 11)

With this in mind we invite the reader to turn to Gareth Morgan's (1986) suggestion that students of organizational behavior should 'read organizations' rather than analyze them. To facilitate reading an organization, Morgan suggests the use of 'metaphors' that imply:

> A way of thinking and a way of seeing that pervade how we understand our world generally ... By using different metaphors to understand the complex and paradoxical character of organizational life, we are able to manage and design organizations in ways that we may not have thought possible before. (Morgan, 1986: 12–13)

As we've previously stated, organizations are not fixed, social entities. They are, in fact, organic, changing to fulfill a particular goal, adjusting to economic demands, etc. For this reason, a 'reader' of an organization cannot fixate on one metaphor over another, but use the metaphor instead to find meaning in one incident or an approach to problem-solving. For example, Morgan suggests that organizations can function like machines, where productivity, management hierarchy, and employees function in a rigid, mechanistic way; behavior can be replicated over and over again, because employees are merely the extensions of the machines they use. Another metaphor describes the organization as a living organism complete with an open system comprised of subsystems that can adapt to their environments and humans who can be motivated. How then do we attempt to understand the client organization for which a product is being designed?

How to 'read' the client organization

Keeping in mind the advice to 'read' organizations rather than 'analyze' them, how, then, does an information designer better understand the client organization for which the information system is being developed? Complex social settings require flexible and multiple research and analytical methods. We suggest a number of strategies that can be employed as appropriate by a designated group within the design team.

A simple place, although superficial, to begin is by examining how the client organization portrays itself officially through an organization chart. Mostly likely the organization is divided into smaller and more manageable units that make the work of the organization compatible with that accomplished in other units. Classical writers in management

Figure 3.1 Example of an organization chart

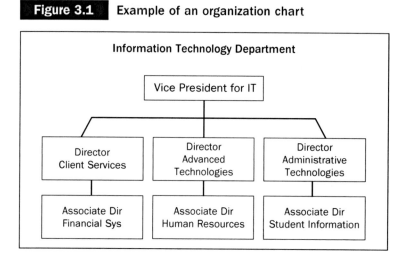

viewed organizations as stable structures, almost always arranged in hierarchical fashion, with the power and vision flowing in an orderly manner from the individuals at the top of the organization to those below. What can the structure of the organization tell the information designer about how the information product under design will be used? The organization chart informs the design team of the variety of production units or functions existing within the client organization. For example, take the organization chart of an academic department of information resources and technology shown in Figure 3.1.

When the design team has located appropriate organization charts they are better prepared to understand the workflow, the centers of power and authority, as well as some of the diversification of tasks. The next step is to explore the organizational context within which future users of the information system work. Of course, there is much more to understanding an organization than how it is structured on 'paper.' The organization chart, however, provides a document on which to focus discussion with organizational members.

Most organizational members will confirm that while the organizational structure often dictates lines of authority, responsibility, and function, there often are other equally (or more) important lines of communication and power and influence. The importance of understanding the context of information retrieval is examined by authors Cool and Spink (2002) who describe the context as including 'cognitive, social and other factors related to a person's tasks, goals and intentions ...' (p. 606). By devoting time to gather data about the workings of an organization, critical information can be discovered concerning the context in which an information system will be used. The steps provided in the guide illustrated in Figure 3.2 suggest several simple places to begin.

Organizational behavioral studies have demonstrated that on the surface individual organizations may appear to be similar, but upon closer examination each organization exhibits its own unique culture: rules for behavior,

Figure 3.2   Guide to understanding client organizations

1. Locate an organization chart.

2. Interview individuals from 'all levels' of the organization to discuss the organizational hierarchy.

3. Ask respondents to identify seats of power and sources of information, both formal and informal.

4. Request a copy of an annual report or other documentation discussing the work of the organization.

5. Collect other 'artifacts' of the organization (T-shirts, brochures, pens, examples of employee awards, etc.).

communication, celebration, ethics, etc. Taking a general systems view of an organization allows the design team to move from a macro view of the client organization to the micro view, where interaction among dependent social and work systems reveals more information about the organizational context. The following section considers the ecology of organizations and the use of qualitative research methods to systematically collect data that will contribute to a thick and rich description of the client organization.

Ecology of organizations

When we think of ecology we envisage the investigation of how various species of plants and animals interact with each other and with the environment. To consider the ecology of an organization we must think of the organization as an organic system. Taking an ecological view of an organization requires the investigator to examine all interacting social systems that make the organization what it is. In this instance, we use the term 'systems' to include all systems (social, managerial, communication, etc.) and not just information or technology systems.

Ecological study ranges from examining the simplest level to a level so complex that detailed studies can take years to record. For the purposes of this discussion we will view an organization as a community of interacting groups of individuals who make up an organization. Let's consider, for example, an organization such as the University of Texas system in which these authors work in a school on one campus out of 15 distributed across the state of Texas. If we were to look more closely at each campus we would find a number of similarities and dissimilarities. Table 3.1 presents a few examples of these differences.

Table 3.1 Organizational differences

Similarities	Dissimilarities
■ Presidents and vice-presidents ■ Colleges, schools, and departments ■ Large and small libraries ■ Multiple campuses ■ Bus and transportation system ■ Use same online accounting system	■ Only graduate degree programs ■ Only one library ■ One campus ■ Collaborative educational program with other educational entities ■ Unique online information systems (library, Web, portals)

When examined from a macro view the different universities may indeed look very similar, after all they are all part of the University of Texas system. On closer examination, we see that there are many, many differences that demand special attention from an information design team. The data-gathering tools of ethnography can be employed by the information system designer to study an organization from an ecological perspective.

Real-world examples and analysis

Let's consider a couple of real-world examples. At the time of this publication, the University of Texas at Austin, a publicly supported university, had 50,000 students (undergraduate and graduate), 3,000 faculty and 18,000 staff members. This one campus includes 16 colleges and schools, as well as seven museums and 17 libraries. A current university project is to digitize and make accessible some of the many cultural and intellectual treasures of the institution. The online system named Utopia began as a project of the university's Information Technology Services Department. The goal of the project was to:

... create the universal university, the pathway to information for all people, regardless of location, resources or technical skills. We will offer knowledge that is accessible, usable, and authoritative. And in so doing, ... transform the role of universities in our society.

In an ideal world using the tools of ethnography the design team would begin to examine the culture of this organization. What are the primary means of communication? What is unique about its rules of behavior (both formal and implied)? Are there existing models for information sharing and collaboration? How do other units, academic and administrative, interact with and use the organization's existing libraries and digitized collections? How might the design team for the Utopia project determine the information needs of its prospective users (the citizens of Texas)?

The use of ethnographic research methods has become increasingly important in the design of information systems.

A major point in ethnographically inspired approaches is that work is a socially organized activity where the actual behavior differs from how it is described by those who do it. (Simonsen and Kensing, 1997: 82)

Let us now consider how an information system design team can use ethnographic research tools to better understand the client organization.

Understanding organizations using ethnographic research tools

Ethnographic research methods can facilitate enhanced understanding of an organization or social group by gathering data that will contribute to describing the organizational context for information system designers. Note that we are not suggesting that the system design group make a trip to the local outfitter for safari attire but instead apply the simple but revealing tools of ethnography to 'read' the organization for which the information system is being designed. With these tools the information design team can create more realistic and functional scenarios to 'imagine' the variety of ways in which a system will be used.

While a variety of qualitative research methods offer alternatives for data collection and validation, it is the use of the flexible, intuitive, and experienced human research instrument that is unique about these techniques (Rice-Lively, 1997: 245). Ethnographic research methods, however, appear to be well suited to building a holistic view of the client organization within a particular setting. The term ethnography is derived from the Greek 'ethnos' (people or cultural group) and graphic, literally, means the 'writing of the people.' A sub-discipline of descriptive anthropology, ethnography 'refers to a social scientific description of a people and the cultural basis of their peoplehood' (Peacock, 1986, as cited in Denzin and Lincoln, 2002: 40).

Popular publications such as *National Geographic* or television programs such as the topics explored on the Discovery Channel often create the impression that ethnography exists only in the domain of anthropologists studying the culture of remote or obscure social groups. Ethnographers can spend years and years seeking to understand and describe the culture of a social group. The application of ethnographic research strategies can also satisfy some of the more casual goals in understanding a client organization. Among the ethnographic data collection methods are: observation, interviews, and focus groups. Each of these methods will be discussed in the following sections.

Observation as a data-gathering method

Clearly, the designer of an information system is not conducting a massive, long-term research project. The goal of employing a data collection method such as observation is to begin to piece together the context of information use within the client organization. While observation is not unique to ethnographic research methods, it is a fundamental tool to seek meaning within an organization. There are two types of observation: detached and participant observation.

The detached observer minimizes interaction with the social group being observed, attempting to be unobtrusive and influencing the setting as little as possible. On the other hand, embracing the role of a participant observer gives the design team an opportunity to experience the real world of members of the client organization. The team goes to an environment in which the proposed system will be introduced. They interact within the environment like others in the same setting. There are some differences, however. The team members only observe or do the same things as those people. The argument here is that if you do not do what those people are doing, how can you get the same feeling as they do? But we also need to consider professional requirements and safety considerations in organizational settings such as hospitals and factories where professional employees are highly skilled and safety issues are critical. Therefore the design team must take these issues into account.

The methods mentioned, while widely used, have their pros and cons. The data collection method employed should be determined by the purpose of the system design, project timeline, budgets, personnel, etc. No single method alone can collect the desired data. Each method, however, will contribute valuable information to guide the design team in their creation of scenarios that contribute to an understanding of the users and their tasks.

The researcher must cultivate the skills of seeing detailed, specific incidents, while never loosing what we will call the 'helicopter view', i.e. the view to be had while hovering over an event or place. Observations are conducted unobtrusively but not clandestinely. Someone within the organization should give permission for the observations to take place and be told what purpose the observations will serve. To accumulate meaningful data, the observer must not depend upon one's memory for these scenes but keep detailed, 'rich and thick' descriptive notes of what is being seen. Consider the example provided in Figure 3.3. The example, while brief, enables the reader to visualize the setting and people within the setting and as well as discover some of the techniques users of this online system have developed to overcome apparent deficiencies within the system itself.

Data collected through observations can provide a researcher with information on how a space is used. The keen observer will take note of how occupants of that space interact with each other and with the space – more specifically, in our case, how the people interact with the online system. Observation enables the researcher to gather a variety of perspectives or degrees of involvement with the situation being observed. Observation also contributes a sense of 'reality' to the research setting while studying behavior within a natural setting (Gorman and Clayton, 1997: 105). Observation alone, however, does not allow the researcher to explore why those observed are doing what they are doing. In the scenario provided in Figure 3.3 it appears that some users of the online catalog prefer the less exact search strategy using Google to the more traditional, structured although specific search strategy of the online catalog. The scenario doesn't, however, tell the researcher

Figure 3.3 Observations of users of an academic library's online catalogue

Goal: *In preparation for a redesign of the user interface of the library's online catalog, the researcher seeks to understand the public use of the client organization's search interface with the library's online catalog.*

The main area where library visitors search the library's online catalog is a brightly lit cavernous room with 20 octagonal shaped counter-height tables, each hosting four computer workstations. A handful of individuals scattered around the room are quietly typing messages into the computers. There are several people who appear to be students, sporting jeans, T-shirts, flip-flops and/or jogging shoes, and all are wearing a backpack of some type. A few computer users appear to be faculty or professionals, some dressed casually like the students and others in business attire.

As I wander around the room, attempting to discern the goals (while not noting the specific content) of the individuals tapping queries into the computer, I notice that some users are actually searching using the online catalog's structured search engine while other users who admit to be looking for books within the library are using general Internet search engines such as Google or Yahoo. When asked why they were looking for a specific library book using Google, several respondents indicated that they weren't having any luck with the online catalog's search engine and were actually coming up with more useful titles using Google.

why this is so. Interviews with individuals in a research or organizational setting speeds up the researcher's response to the 'why' of particular behavior within a setting.

Interviews with members of the client organization

Corrine Glesne describes interviewing as 'the process of getting words to fly' (Glesne, 1999: 67). In all qualitative research the respondent to researcher questions is considered the expert, because it is the respondent who has the information the researcher needs in order to understand the 'why' of behavior within an organizational or social setting. Interviews are most often conducted in a face-to-face setting where trust can be established, thus enabling mutual exploration of a topic.

The design team can collect detailed feedback from interviews. Before conducting interviews, the design team must develop interview guidelines and train interviewers to better accommodate consistency and minimize the variability between interviews. The interview guidelines can be established based on the results of the data analysis and questionnaire. Among other things the interview guidelines should include of a list of questions, the interview procedure, and how to set up the interview environment.

As noted in the previous chapter in the discussion of questionnaires, interviews are only as good as the questions that are asked. Time and thought must be given to the development of questions. Every question must evolve from the overall goals of an inquiry, as well as be grounded in the social or organizational setting. Patton (1990) suggests that questions should focus on topics about which the respondent is an expert: feelings, behavior, opinions, experience, etc. When refining the interview, you should read through each question and confirm that each question is seeking information about something you need to know.

When conducted properly, interviews offer a more personal orientation to data collection. The researcher must both acknowledge personal expectations for the answers to questions and make every effort to record (either through note-taking or a recording device) the exact words of a respondent. Survey questions offer another interview technique, even though this data collection method, while useful for baseline or demographic data about a respondent, often yields only superficial data. Without direct face-to-face follow-up the researcher cannot pursue information behind the answers nor investigate unanswered questions.

Since oral communication can be highly subjective and interpreted differently, the team may want to use a recorder to capture the questions that have been asked and to prevent any interference between the interviewer and interviewee. The team can also audio- or video-record interviews for data analysis. Videotaping is desirable when the interviewees' actions are part of the study. For better data management and analysis, software is available. Among popular products are the QSR offerings N6 and the latest version of Nud*ist, a program that allows access to data and the automation of clerical tasks. Another QSR product, NVivo, is designed for researchers who need to combine subtle coding with qualitative linking, shaping, searching, and modeling, and may be used when working with complex rich-text data, such as multimedia, in order to conduct deep levels of analysis (for more information see *http://www.qsrinternational.com/software.htm*). Another popular data analysis software program is The Ethnograph©, a product from Qualis Research. This program allows researchers to import and analyze large quantities of textual data (see *http://www.qualisresearch.com/*). These and other software programs are also useful for document analysis when reviewing the transcripts of focus groups, another approach to 'asking questions' discussed in the next section.

Focus groups as a way to gather data

Data collection is also possible through the use of focus groups – small groups of six to ten people. The method is preferred when the team wants to discover the social interactions from a group with several common features. Remember that the common features are identified by the design team and are relevant to the system design. A focus group can be formed on the basis of geographic location, employment position, gender, computer skills, etc.

By using the focus group, the design team can collect data about 'group wisdom.' The typical focus group involves six to ten people and is chaired by a host, with the meeting lasting about 2–3 hours. The focus group came into being in the late 1930s as a non-directive way to interview individuals. They were created to some extent to remove the influence of the interviewer (Krueger and Casey, 2000). Focus groups provide access to the attitudes and perceptions of individuals interacting in a social setting. Asking for an opinion about a service or an attitude toward something in a one-on-one interview assumes that the respondent has the answer. In the social setting of a focus group, individuals resonate to the words of others, triggering responses that might not emerge in a one-on-one interview. The members of the focus group can contribute personal opinions on the system first. As the discussion proceeds, interaction among the members enables them to share more ideas and gives the design team more insight. However, the host must be aware that such an interaction may be a result of peer pressure. When such a doubt occurs, the host should slow down the discussion and clarify any questionable statements to avoid going off in a wrong direction.

Recording facilities are needed in the focus group since several people are involved and the data is rich. The recording facilities also help the host concentrate on leading the discussion. Like interviews, the host should have a list of questions, discussion guidelines, and training beforehand. Crafting well-conceived, purposeful questions for focus groups is critical. Use open-ended questions that avoid 'yes' or 'no' answers. We often envision a focus group as a deliberate gathering of people sitting in a circle behind a one-way glass window discussing the pros and cons of a particular product, program, service, or issue.

Focus groups usually are lead by one researcher who asks the questions and another who keeps notes, observes, and enriches the content of a recorded session with descriptive information. The participants are more or less homogenous, but representing various opinions. For example, in the scenario described in Figure 3.3 the group observed includes students from different study disciplines. Were several of these individuals selected to participate in a focus group they would be considered homogenous because they are all students, but they would also contribute a variety of perspectives because they represent the information-seeking needs of business, biology, English literature, and information science.

The above data collection methods (observation, interviews, and focus groups) can be supplemented by the collection of artifacts from the client organization. In this case, an artifact might include flyers or brochures describing the client organization, pins, ball caps, T-shirts, etc. and all will contribute to an understanding of the culture and focus of the client organization. The traditional ethnographer's field journal, whether a physical spiral-bound notebook, a PDA, or even a laptop computer, is a useful way to capture unformed impressions, questions, topics to pursue further, ideas or opinions. A field journal in whatever form will guide the researcher in making sense of the data collected.

Once data has been collected case studies can be written as yet another strategy to explore the context of a particular user.

Use of case studies

We define *case studies* broadly here. In order to construct scenarios in which different users (actors) and their actions take place, the design team must employ various methods to capture such data for the system requirements. The design team should keep one thing in mind all the time: we have to use as many methods as possible to understand users and their actions. We recommend the following methods to study users as a starting point, but they should not prevent the design team from exploring other methods while time and budget allow.

Document analysis is an important method to initiate user studies. Earlier we discussed how the design team could get employee information for an organization-wide system. In this case, the design team can get details of the distribution of employees, their skills, educational backgrounds, etc. This is the easiest situation since the information exists and the design team only needs to know how to extract and interpret the information to establish an initial understanding of the users.

If information on the users is not available, the design team may need to purchase or search for information. Some statistical data can be found online or in reference materials. However, the team needs to review the statistical data carefully before interpreting it. For customer information, the team may have to purchase such data from marketing firms.

This also provides a lesson for the design team on collecting user information for the future. With the power of computing technologies, many computer-based systems can set up parameters to collect user information. For example, web log and tracking software is able to record each user's actions on a website such as the number of sites visited, visit time, links, etc. However, some software provides only limited functionality so the team must be familiar with the software and the purpose of the log analyses. Although there are numerous examples a few popular products are NetTracker (*http://www.sane.com*) and WebTrends (*http://www.webtrends.com*). For an interesting comparison of these and other tools see *http://www.cryer.co.uk/resources/websitetracking.htm*.

Organizations must also be understood in the ways that they make sense of information and events. How an organization and its members adapt to and respond to changes in their organizational environment leads the information design team to consider not only the ecological perspectives of an organization, but also the organization from a cognitive approach.

Sense-making as a cognitive tool to understand organizations

Sense-making is used as both a theory and a practice. Brenda Dervin, a communications scholar, and Karl Weick, an industrial psychologist, are leaders in sense-making research. Weick explains sense-making as involving both individual and group sense-making processes and behaviors. The concept is grounded in theories of communication, information, social cognition, and constructivism and can be evidenced in individual and group efforts to understand or grasp a situation or information. Choo (1998) explores sense-making as part of the 'knowing organization' – how the organization uses information for 'sense-making, knowledge creating, and decision making'. These are all highly interconnected activities that contribute to our understanding of the client organization (p. 3).

During a 'sense-making episode' the user tries to construct meaning by bridging gaps of understanding between what they experience and their past 'image' of a similar experience. The situation is novel and there appears to be a discrepancy between what is expected and what is observed. To make sense, the sense-maker must take some deliberate initiative to understand. For example, users of a new software product often experience 'gaps' in their understanding, sometimes due to a bug in the program itself (or a 'feature' depending upon whether you are the user or the software designer), or to unclear interface design, or to any number of other reasons. When the user receives an unexpected response to a query where do they turn to make sense of their experience and find out how to proceed? Do they pull out the documentation that accompanies the product? Do they put in a call to a help desk? Or do they ask a knowledgeable colleague?

Starbuck and Milliken (1988) outline several distinct aspects of sense-making that include comprehending, understanding, explaining, attributing, extrapolating, and predicting. Sense-making is critical to organizational survival because ambiguous information must be used to shape directions and to make decisions. While there may be multiple interpretations of information, Choo reminds us that organizations create 'a network of shared meanings and interpretations that contribute to the social order, temporal continuity, and contextual clarity for members to coordinate and relate their actions' (1998: 79).

Summary

The task of exploring the client organization from both an ecological approach as well as a cognitive approach provides information designers with access to how the organization operates, the types of users, and their information and production needs as they relate to the information system. Using ethnographic research methods, as well as other qualitative research techniques such as focus groups, observation, and interviews, allows the design team to get closer to the actual work practices of the client organization. More importantly, the exercise of gathering this type of data will more realistically inform the creation of the product use scenarios we will discuss in Part 2 of this book.

References

Choo, C.W. (1998) *The Knowing Organization: How Organizations Use Information to Construct Meaning, Create Knowledge, and Make Decisions.* New York: Oxford University Press.

Erickson, T. (1995) 'Notes on design practice: stories and prototypes as catalysts,' in J.M. Carroll (ed.), *Scenario-Based Design: Envisioning Work and Technology in System Development.* New York: John Wiley & Sons, pp. 37–58.

Glesne, C. (1999) *Becoming Qualitative Researchers: An Introduction,* 2nd edn. New York: Longman, pp. 67–94.

Krueger, R.A. and Casey, M.A. (2000) *Focus Groups: A Practical Guide for Applied Research.* Thousand Oaks, CA: Sage.

Simonsen, J. and Kensing, F. (1997) 'Ethnography in contextual design,' *Communication of the ACM*, 40 (7): 82–8.

Starbuck, W.H. and Milliken, F.J. (1988) 'Executives' perceptual filters: what they notice and how they make sense,' in D.C. Hambrick (ed.), *The Executive Effect: Concepts and Methods for Studying Top Managers*. Greenwich, CT: JAI Press, pp. 35–65.

Communicating with stakeholders

We often complain that the left hand does not know what the right hand is doing. Communication is the key to a well-defined and established communication network that can prevent such a mistake. The design team needs to identify with whom they should communicate, how to keep those people informed, and how to create a usable space for interaction and feedback. The communication network assures the construction of user-centered scenarios, and the provision for each team member of user data to perform his or her duties. Ideally, this will enable administrators to monitor key dates of the project; team members can share data effectively, test prototypes, complete the final version; and users can anticipate available products.

Know who should get involved

Designing an information system requires teamwork. The design team consists not only of its members but also administrators and users. Practitioners and researchers in the area of computer-supported cooperative work (CSCW) have recognized a social-technical gap over the last decade (Ackerman, 2002). Organizations attempting to implement an information system should recognize such challenges. Some causes of the social-technical gap are individual ignorance and organizational conflict. The design team needs to build a common ground to resolve such ignorance and conflict.

The design team must identify all stakeholders involved in the new information system. For a small organization, each stakeholder should be able to communicate with the design team via different channels. For a big organization, the design team must know how to select appropriate delegates from different user groups. These procedures vary from organization to organization and rules cannot be applied universally. The broader the representation of the stakeholders, the better chance for a successful implementation of the new information system.

When employees and users become comfortable with routine procedures, new requirements and tasks from the new information system are likely to stir up discomfort and resistance. This is especially true when such requirements and tasks are not initiated by employees and users. They need to have 'communication outlets' to express their concerns so that the design team and administration can address employee and user concerns and work to ease anxiety. Norman (1993) pointed out that *distributed cognition* supports individuals to interact with each other and to carry out innovative ideas. We call this approach, *distributed wisdom and power.*

The distribution of communication accumulates *wisdom* from all stakeholders, who have the *power* to share their experience and knowledge. Meanwhile, the shared experience and knowledge *empower* other stakeholders to gain knowledge. However, the distribution can be positive and negative. As stakeholders become knowledgeable and informed about the new information system, they may be more willing to accept the new system. Unfortunately, such information sharing may cause unnecessary reward-fighting among employees and unwanted external business competition. In addition, employees may fight over rewards while implementing the new information system. 'Who is going to get the credit?' they may ask. 'Will the new information system render a particular department obsolete?'

In business competition, for example, other companies may learn about the new information system and launch their own new products to counter it. The design team needs to work with administrators to make information accessible to the stakeholders and establish a control mechanism for information sharing and protection.

Advisory committee

To facilitate the implementation of the new information system, an advisory committee is needed, especially in a large organization. The role of the advisory committee is to advocate a new vision, mission, and directions for the system. Its members are visionary people with high positions (internal and external). External and internal committee members help to break barriers between domains, departments, and offices in order to bring all stakeholders to the table when developing a new information system. The committee also performs as a catalyst to promote new knowledge and ideas. It is important to have such a unit in place.

Management committee

The management committee consists of a group of 'doers' while the advisory committee is a group of 'thinkers.' The members of the management committee are visionary people with practical experience and managing ability. Their responsibilities are to implement the system, monitor its progress, and oversee interdepartmental collaborations.

Each member of the management committee can lead a sub-committee of different components: IT, finance and budget, human resources, communications and public relations, etc. These committees have a two-fold function: *sharing the responsibilities* and *educating stakeholders*. Constructing user scenarios is complicated and requires that all departments work together. Committees also help to bridge the boundaries among the departments and change the organizational culture. Some employees may not be aware of their roles and work responsibilities with regard to constructing user scenarios. For example, a marketing representative may not realize that his or her experience with customers is a great asset to the information system design since he or she is the interface between the company and its customers.

Creating a positive atmosphere

The management committee members must create a positive atmosphere in the entire organization, in their own departments, and for customers. The atmosphere encourages all stakeholders to create ideas, and to share and refine them. When all stakeholders talk to each other, a common ground can emerge. The common ground may not be smooth but at least it is visible and fertile for more in-depth discussion.

Changing the organizational culture

Once a positive atmosphere is formed, the organizational culture may begin to change. Stakeholders are motivated to participate in discussion, to get involved in future actions, and to implement the new information system. Such vibrant interactions prompt a constant flow of ideas and keep the stakeholders on the move.

Establishing a reward system

A reward system should be presented at the same time as the organizational change. The purpose of the reward system is to encourage stakeholders to be active and to honor their contributions. The reward can take many forms. For example, customers could get a free T-shirt for filling out a survey, or employees could get a monthly priority parking spot for finishing assignments on time. The reward system must be clear and fair to avoid any internal and external conflict. Rewards should be given to active stakeholders for their valuable contributions.

Strengthening collaboration

The purpose of creating a positive atmosphere, changing the organizational culture, and establishing a reward system is to strengthen collaboration. An open-minded atmosphere and positive organizational changes encourage stakeholders to communicate. Rewards motivate individuals to make contributions and clarify each department's responsibilities. Therefore user scenarios can be constructed by collaboration and the scenarios will be acknowledged by the stakeholders.

Keeping them informed

Information must be visible, timely, effective, and plentiful to the stakeholders. The visibility helps ideas to flow and to be shared. Ideas can be presented as text, graphics, photos, charts, etc. The stakeholders should be encouraged to present their ideas in any format. In order to promote idea sharing, the design team has to investigate how many communication channels are available to stakeholders to present their ideas.

For example, a group of office workers may post their ideas on a bulletin board since they are in the same office. They use sketches, text, charts, and other forms to articulate their ideas. The key is to make ideas *seen* to inspire other stakeholders! Such activities will initiate organizational changes and better communication. For larger organizations, the design team needs to be able to provide adequate communication channels to stakeholders.

When ideas are visible, we have to pursue timely information release and response. We all know that timing is everything. The design team must create a good method of ensuring information delivery. Such a method is related to the selection of information channels.

In the above example of office workers, a physical bulletin or notice board is used as the information channel. The assumption is that the bulletin board is in a highly visible location. Each office worker will notice newly posted ideas and post their reactions instantly. In order to maintain the bulletin board, we need to make sure of the lifecycle of each posting. Each posting should show the date posted, the deadline for feedback, and a removal date. We also need some people to monitor the whole process. The key point is to keep every posting up to date. We can also use some computer-aided programs to monitor time-control. There are many project management programs available on the market. These programs can monitor the progress of the project to meet different deadlines. However, the programs are *just* tools!

When ideas are visible and shared in a timely manner, the effectiveness and sufficiency of this communication can be achieved. Effectiveness is often measured by the speed of communication and interaction among stakeholders. The likelihood of miscommunication can be reduced when stakeholders use different forums to share their ideas. It is important that each stakeholder should feel free to use any appropriate presentation format to express and share ideas. However, achieving effectiveness and sufficiency is environment- and organization-related. The following examples will provide you with some ideas on the implementation of visible and timely information.

E-mail

Most of us make heavy use of e-mail as an important means of communication in both our work and personal lives. However, we also spend a great deal of time deleting or filtering our e-mail. For this reason, many e-mail messages may not ever be read by recipients. Figure 4.1 shows you the

Figure 4.1   Effective e-mail format

From:	Susan Smith <S.Smith@mymail.com>
To:	Project Mailing List
Topic:	Interface Design Version 0.2
Content:	– test site: http://projectA.com/version_0.2/
	– answer an online 5-question survey at the test site
	– finish the test by 3:00 pm, Tuesday, March 20

basics of an effective e-mail message that includes a subject heading, clear and concise content, and a relevant deadline.

To facilitate efficient and sufficient communication be sure to:

- Create a mail list of the stakeholders.

- Describe a clear topic for your e-mail message.

- Make the content short and precise.

- Use the Web as part of your multimedia presentation and you can avoid a wordy description in the content.

- List all required actions.

- Make a deadline for reply.

This procedure will help you communicate with stakeholders more quickly and collect answers from them easily.

Online forum

Today there are many alternatives for creating an online forum: online discussion groups, blog, wikis, etc. The reason for using an online forum is to avoid overwhelming each individual with e-mail and to present an open discussion to a certain group of stakeholders. You can set up a free discussion group with Internet ventures such as Yahoo (see Figure 4.2). For security and privacy concerns, you can put the discussion group within your organization. The discussion group is like a bulletin board where people can post information and react to information that has been posted.

A blog, also called a weblog (associated terms which are self-explanatory include blogger, blogrolling, and blogosphere), is a website (or section of a website) where visitors post their thoughts chronologically (see Figure 4.3). Free blog sites can be found online or you can set up a blog site in your organization for security and privacy concerns.

Figure 4.2 Yahoo's discussion groups

Source: http://groups.yahoo.com

Figure 4.3 Blog

Source: http://blogger.com

Of late wikis have become a popular means of communication and document sharing. 'A wiki is a web application that allows users to add content, as on an Internet forum, but also allows anyone to edit the content. The term wiki also refers to the collaborative software used to create such a website' (Wikipedia, *http://www.wikipedia.org*). Wikis run using wiki software hosted on a web server.

Information packet

The examples discussed above are for the online environment. We also need to consider offline stakeholders and how to present information to them. Information packets can be anything and everything from printed brochures and flyers to CD-ROMs and DVDs. For example, when the design team invents a new device and wants to know how your potential users will use it, they can begin by sending potential users and stakeholders a prototype for testing.

The design team also can use CD-ROMs, DVDs, or other digital media to distribute the information packets. Such digital media can hold massive amounts of information in different formats. For example, suppose you are designing a new library building and want to get feedback from library users. A multimedia information packet can be a useful tool for reaching your audience. You can present the blueprint of the building, pictures of the model, 3D images of the building if possible, and even a video interview of yourself for the audience. In the interview, you guide the audience through the design of the new library building and explain the development of the project. With the digital tools currently available (digital cameras, digital camcorders) and software, you can create digital images and illustrations with a variety of software programs and produce digital videos.

These in-house productions can be very useful and timely and distributed on a DVD or CD-ROM at a relatively low cost. The design team must assemble an information packet using appropriate media to present their ideas clearly and so persuade the stakeholders.

Providing a space for interaction

Informing the stakeholders is one-way communication. Real-time interaction is needed to put all stakeholders on the same page, to discuss agreements and disagreements, and to reach common resolutions on the design of the system. The administration needs to encourage stakeholders to have conversations with the design team to generate a knowledge community.

Meetings

Meetings, if well planned, can be a good forum for important communication and interaction. The design team should choose the meeting size and format wisely. The following are some good examples:

- Town-hall meetings are appropriate when the target users are in a mid-size physical environment such as a small town or a neighborhood. The design team should restrict the number of attendees at the meeting to fewer than 100 to enable in-depth discussion. The meetings should be held at different times and locations to accommodate different stakeholders.

- Focus group meetings should be used when the design team is facing a distinct group of stakeholders with specific concerns. Focus groups should be carefully selected with regard to their characteristics and the purposes of the system.

Teleconferencing

Due to time and geographic limitations, the design team may need to hold meetings via telecommunication:

- *Online chat room.* Many Internet service vendors provide online chat services equipped with video. The chat service can accommodate multiple users simultaneously. Online video chatting enables better interaction among stakeholders to overcome time and geographic barriers.

- *Videoconferencing.* The design team should use videoconferencing when a large group is involved. The number of locations and attendees at each location should be controlled. If you want to have more attendees at each location, the number of locations should be less, or vice versa. By doing so, each attendee can have a chance to express his or her concerns. No observers are needed in a videoconference, as the session can be saved to a video-cassette or other storage media.

On-site visiting

On-site visits are important when the design team needs to observe stakeholders' actions. At the different stages of the system implementation, the team needs to know how stakeholders' actually use the system. On-site observations provide the team with contextual understandings in the stakeholders' environments. The visits should be conducted in conjunction with town hall and focus group meetings.

The team can then generate meeting agendas from on-site observations.

Keeping plans and ideas secure

Intellectual property protection and rights management

Throughout the informing and interaction process, the design team needs to secure intellectual property and rights management. Sensitive data must be protected by passwords and provided only to classified personnel. If the sensitive data is managed by an online system, online transitions of the access activities should be applied to monitor users, amount of data and use time, location, etc. Physical copies of sensitive data should be coded and recalled after meetings.

Content management

Through the informing and interaction process, the design team will develop more ideas from the stakeholders. Tracking ideas and determining their life cycle is important to the design of the system. We will discuss these topics in Chapter 7 on the life cycle of ideas.

The design team needs to acknowledge the stakeholders' privacy. In some cases, the team may need to obtain consent from the stakeholders before any interaction takes place. The stakeholders must know their involvement in the project, the use of their feedback, and possible consequences. When collecting confidential data, the team has to justify the need for such data. For example, the team needs to tell potential meeting attendees if the meeting is being broadcast, so attendees can decide whether they want to be there. The team also has to keep the stakeholders informed of their participation with the progress of the project. Users' confidential data must be protected according to the users' status and the law. In the US, for example, students' academic records are protected by the Family Educational Rights and Privacy Act (FERPA).

Tracking progress

The management committee and group leaders are responsible for tracking the progress of the project. Control mechanisms or tools must be developed based on time, goals, and teams. These mechanisms and tools can be paper- or computer-based depending on the complexity of the project and the stakeholders involved.

For a small project and limited personnel, the design team can use several charts to manage the progress of the project:

- *Time-oriented.* First, all deadlines should be realistically defined. Figure 4.4 shows an example for a six-month project. The design team has to finish the project consisting of three major tasks. A time-oriented chart

Figure 4.4 Time-based project management

Time Tasks	Month 1	Month 2	Month 3	Month 4	Month 5	Month 6
1	━━━	━━━	━━━			
2			━━━	━━━		
3					━━━	━━━

known as a Gantt chart can be used to monitor the progress of the project by displaying the length of a task, the start and finish times, and its relationship to other tasks.

■ *Goal-oriented.* A goal-oriented approach takes a more in-depth look at the tasks. Consequently, more details are needed for monitoring. Figure 4.5 shows how sub-tasks are presented under three major tasks. A goal-oriented chart helps the design team accomplish each task and sub-task in a timely manner.

■ *Team-based.* Suppose, for the same project, four departments are involved. In the team-based approach, the responsibilities of each department – Accounting,

Figure 4.5 Goal-oriented project management

Time / Tasks	Month 1	Month 2	Month 3	Month 4	Month 5	Month 6
1	▬▬▬▬▬	▬▬▬▬▬	▬▬▬▬▬			
1.1	—					
1.2		—				
1.3			—			
2		▬▬▬▬▬	▬▬▬▬▬	▬▬▬▬▬		
2.1		—	—			
2.2				—		
3					▬▬▬▬▬	▬▬▬▬▬
3.1					—	
3.2						—

Figure 4.6 Team-based project management

Time / Teams	Month 1	Month 2	Month 3	Month 4	Month 5	Month 6
Accounting	(Task 1.1)					(Task 3.2)
PR		(Task 2.1)			(Task 3.1)	
IT		(Task 1.3)	(Task 2.1)			
Legal				(Task 2.2)		

Public Relations (PR), Information Technology (IT) – and Legal are specified (see Figure 4.6). In some cases, subdivisions or individual employees may be identified in terms of their responsibilities.

The three charts support each other's function and the design team can add appropriate linking methods to reinforce project management. The team can also find commercial project management software for large-scale projects. Either paper- or computer-based tools can be used to track the progress of the project based on the three approaches.

Summary

The system design team must use appropriate and effective communication techniques to reach different groups of stakeholders under the leadership of an advisory committee and management committee. The use of various communication techniques should be based on how to involve stakeholders in the development of the information system, to create a friendly environment for idea sharing, and to keep stakeholders informed of the progress of the system. The techniques should also enable the design team to monitor the key dates of the project, allow team members to share data effectively, and permit stakeholders to anticipate available products.

References

Ackerman, M.S. (2002) 'The intellectual challenge of CSCW: the gap between social requirements and technical feasibility', in J.M. Carroll (ed.), *Human–Computer Interaction in the New Millennium.* New York: ACM Press, pp. 303–24.

Norman, D.A. (1993) *Things That Make Us Smart.* Reading, MA: Addison-Wesley.

Wiki (2005) *Wikipedia: The free encyclopedia.* Retrieved August 21, from *http://www.wikipedia.org.*

Part 2
Theoretical Practices

Managing scenario design projects and knowledge

This chapter will explore project and knowledge management principles. Basic project management tenets will inform the practical steps to manage your design project as well as the 'knowledge' and expertise that are accrued during the project. To begin the exploration we will define terms as used in this context. Furthermore, we will consider how to employ the above principles, and guide you in determining and monitoring short- and long-term goals for communication and management of information and knowledge. The primary focus of the chapter is to offer tools to guide the planning, development and management of an information design project, a project that begins with the information needs and context of the information user. For this reason, we will not explore management theory as such. Let us begin with an exploration of the meanings of the words as we use them in this discussion.

What is management?

No doubt the word management conjures up different meanings and has a variety of implications for each of us. For this reason, let us briefly discuss the term in the context of planning and implementing an information design project.

Understanding the word management, as it affects the concepts of 'knowledge' and 'project' in the context of this discussion, is critical to this chapter. Management also implies that some task or range of tasks must be accomplished. To accomplish these tasks requires planning and coordinating the involvement of people and the use of resources (money, time, durable goods, etc.) with the goal of completing a task. Management implies that someone has been given (or has taken) the role of coordinating, communicating, facilitating, directing, mentoring, and monitoring. The professional literature provides abundant examples of management theory, models, practice, and competencies.

Who and what will be managed?

Proceeding from this rather superficial definition of 'management' we now focus attention on what those of you reading this text will be managing: information design projects. As in any project, your first concern will be the management of the people who are employed in the design project. Members of the project team will bring knowledge, expertise, and experience to the endeavor. Second, as you have probably already observed, the techniques to create scenarios for information design, outlined thus far, will generate a tremendous amount of data for the project design team's use. How will the team manage and make intelligent use of this accumulation of information? How might the design team mine the expertise, insights, and observations gathered? As this chapter title implies, understanding and employing a knowledge management process and/or system is essential to the information design and project management process. Finally, this chapter will explore the theoretical and practical definitions of both knowledge management and project management, as well as the relevance of these two concepts and strategies to the information design process (see Figure 5.1).

So where do we begin the discussion? Should you first consult project management guidelines, or should you apply basic planning strategies? If either of the above, are you then in a position to manage the 'knowledge' being generated by the project? A simple answer to this query is that preparing for project and knowledge management requires that you 'jump in' and 'grab hold' of whatever you can. The process of managing is a circular one with everything moving and interacting at the same time, and with all components sharing overlapping contingencies. For this reason, we have chosen to explore the management process in the following order: general planning strategies, project and time management, and knowledge management.

Figure 5.1 The management process

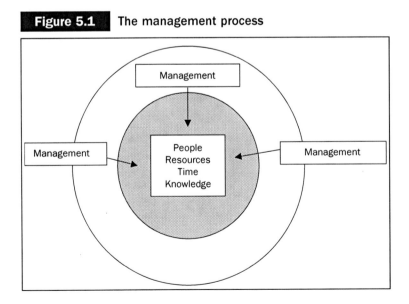

Strategic planning and goal setting

Where are you?

The first step of any planning process is to determine 'where you are.' As discussed in previous chapters, conducting a 'needs assessment' informs the project team of 'where' a particular project (or the client organization) is with regard to the project. To develop project goals and objectives, an assessment of the needs of the client organization must be made. Systematic collection and analysis of data must be conducted. A thorough inventory of internal statistics, services, the nature of operations (efficient or inefficient), and other programs and activities informs the needs assessment. In addition to the internal evaluation, the needs assessment also should include external factors such as non-user or potential client attitudes toward the organization or program, the plans and goals of the parent institution, the economic outlook, and so on. Consider the scenario outlined in Figure 5.2.

As we have recommended in previous chapters, a needs assessment can employ methods such as: surveys of users and non-users, interviews, focus groups, and analyses of demographics (of potential users). The process of conducting a thorough needs assessment and the subsequent development of a list of the implications for the project of the various strengths and weaknesses will shape the information design project in important ways. Does the project team have a methodology to prioritize the importance and complexity of the needs to inform the product's functionality? Prioritizing 'needs' will assist the project team members as they attempt to manage data collection and to assess the relevance of data to the design. Such efforts will prevent the data from dominating or

Figure 5.2   Management case study: where are you?

Web portal off the mark!

Web portals have served to provide a common gateway into the web resources of large organizations. A large university in the US decided that it had to develop a web portal to serve its faculty, students, staff, alumni, and prospective students and faculty. A deadline for the grand opening of the portal was set and the project team began development of the user interface, the selection of content, and the design of the look and feel of the gateway project. However, due to the tight development schedule there was no time to analyze current web usage statistics, to conduct focus groups to collect options for content, or to test the design and interface with prospective users. The project team completed the project on schedule, but the reception by the user community was lukewarm. Among the comments were the following. Why did they include this particular information? How do I find a list of courses? Where do I pay my bills? How can I find an e-mail address for my instructor? In sum, by not making time to collect data and conduct a needs assessment, the project team created a portal based on what they *thought* their users might need, and not one based upon existing data and feedback from the user community.

holding up the planning process. It is important, instead, to view this step as a means to an end.

The collection of data related to past (and current) activities within the client organization will guide decision-making about system functionality to support future activities. Once the data from the needs assessment have been collected the design team must look for information that may challenge long-held assumptions and for changes in user expectations and trends in services. Perhaps the team should also investigate what comparable organizations and programs are doing in the way of similar services and activities. As we have previously noted, there are many levels of need. The needs assessment should provide information so that the major problems in the organization are identified. In summary, the needs assessment guides understanding of 'where we are' on a project.

The next step to any planning process is to determine 'where you want to be!'

Where do you want to be?

To answer the question 'where do you want to be?' you must understand and be able to articulate the project mission or vision statement. The vision statement in essence articulates an inspiring summary of the dreams of the project team concerning the future. Consider for example the vision statement for a university information and research portal project shown in Figure 5.3.

One manager noted that an organization or project's mission should be brief enough for every member of the

Figure 5.3 Example of project mission and vision

> ### Portal Mission and Vision
>
> We aim to provide access for every citizen via a personalized Internet window to the resources of the university's libraries, collections, museums, and much more. The portal aims to bring the university's treasures into every home and business in the state.

group to repeat it without much thought – in short, it should be clear, brief, and to the point.

Developing goals and objectives

The next step in the planning process is to develop the goals and objectives of the project. The goals and objectives should flow from the vision and mission statement. A goal is timeless and not measurable, while an objective is concrete, specific, and measurable with a timeline (e.g. 'by the end of the fiscal year 75 per cent of all projects will be using online planning tools'). Tasks or strategies outline how the objective will be accomplished (see Figure 5.4).

Ongoing evaluation of the planning process

All too frequently organizations become so absorbed in crafting finely developed goals and objectives that they fail

Figure 5.4 Model of purpose of vision, mission, goals, and objectives

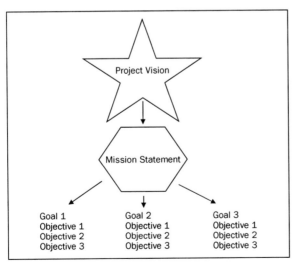

to incorporate criteria for ongoing evaluation of the plan. There are four criteria for evaluating the major areas of the planning process.

- *Goal relatedness* – how does each activity of the project fit into the overall goals for the organization?
- *Feasibility* – what is the potential for a project activity to be successful?
- *Efficiency* – will this course of action optimize results rather than another course of action?
- *Effectiveness or impact.*

With a thoughtful and clearly articulated strategic plan in place, the project team should now consider another important management tool: project management.

Project management principles

This section will explore basic project management principles and illustrate how they relate to knowledge management, as well as their place in the entire information design process.

What is a project?

A project has a beginning and an end. It can be both long and short term. 'A project is a discrete set of activities performed in a logical sequence to attain a specific result' (Kliem and Ludin, 1998: 4). Many of us manage projects without giving much thought to the complexity of what we are doing. For example, you may decide that you want to create a new look in your living room. To begin the project you determine the ultimate goal of the renovation. Is it just a touch-up or rearranging the furniture, or do you want a whole new look? If your goal is the latter, then you must determine what you want to do (paint, new furniture, flooring?), what you can afford (planning a budget is an important aspect of project management), who is going to do the work, and when you want the project to be completed. Answering questions such as these is the first step to a definition of the scope of your project.

Before beginning the project, the project team must define the project in such a way that every member of the project team understands the project's goals and objectives. What are the agreed upon deliverables? What resources are necessary to complete the project and have these resources been provided? If so, clearly delineate these resources in terms of people, money, space, and time. Clarify the constraints and challenges to completing the project, as well as outline and agree upon a timeframe.

Setting project goals and objectives

Usually, the first two questions asked when setting goals and objectives are 'where are we?' and 'where do we want to be?' Using scenarios and understanding the 'context' of an information design project is integral to understanding the 'needs' of the stakeholders. Knowing the 'needs' of information system users informs the project team of 'where we are' (or the client organization is) with regard to the project. As discussed in Chapter 3, systematic collection of data concerning individual and organizational use of the information system to be designed will involve the collection and analysis of internal statistics, other services, the nature of operations (whether they are efficient or inefficient), as well as consideration of related programs and activities. In addition to the internal evaluation, data collection should consider external factors such as non-user or potential client attitudes toward the organization or program, plans, and goals of the parent institution, the economic outlook, and so on.

The 'where we want to be' element of setting goals and objectives shapes the project mission or vision statement. The vision statement in essence is an inspiring summary of the dreams of the project team concerning the future. As noted above, the next step is to develop the goals and objectives of the project. The goals and objectives should flow from the mission statement. A goal is timeless and not measurable. An objective, on the other hand, is concrete, specific, and measurable with a timeline (e.g. 'by September 2005, 75 per cent of the project will be completed'). Tasks or strategies outline the steps required to accomplish each objective.

The next planning step is the identification of the project team and project manager. The project manager, as well as every team member, must have defined and clearly understood roles. Once the team is formed, they must develop and agree upon a vision for the project, so that every project team member can explain not only the vision for the project, but also the project's the goals and objectives. We have already discussed in previous chapters the conducting of a needs assessment and the clarification of the purpose of the project, as well as the identification of tools and techniques to schedule and track the progress on task completion and so on. As noted in Chapter 4 the establishment of clear lines of communication both with members of the project team as well as with the stakeholders is essential to the success of the project.

Finally, the project team must agree with the primary client upon criteria for evaluating project success. Have measures been established to manage the quality of each task completion? Who has responsibility for this? What is the implementation schedule? Is there a plan for ongoing evaluation and adaptation of the deliverable?

Any sizeable project will generate enormous amounts of new information and knowledge. It is insufficient to implement the best strategies of project management without a plan to collect and manage the 'knowledge' that is relevant to the project. The following section will explore the rationale and techniques for managing project information and knowledge.

Knowledge management defined, again

The authors join our readers in the quest for the most useful and understandable definition of 'knowledge management' (KM). Definitions of KM exist in both the scholarly and popular literature. As is often the case, however, the business community and the academic community have yet to concur on a definition of KM. Is KM a product, a system, a process, or a technology? Or is KM all, some, or none of these? We might add that the common strategy of performing a quick Google™ search for spelling, definitions, and background doesn't clear things up. In an exploration of KM curriculum development Michael Koenig (1999) traces the history of the KM movement from 'intellectual capital' and business process re-engineering to other descriptors such as 'knowledge sharing' and 'knowledge networking.' A look at the popular business literature draws a rather different picture. 'Knowledge management is a solid concept that fell in with the wrong company ... software companies, to be precise' (Berkman, 2001). Berkman goes on to describe KM as 'the concept that one of the most valuable corporate assets is the experience and expertise floating round inside employees' heads.' Knowledge management is indeed a puzzle. Most of the research literature discusses KM 'frameworks, approaches, and methodologies' (Ergazakis et al., 2002). Authors Thomas, Kellogg, and Erickson (2001) develop a convincing argument that KM is something more than 'capturing, organizing, and retrieving information' (p. 863), but is inextricably bound up with human cognition and social context.

In Chapter 3 we considered how the information design process must also include the perspectives of individuals and organizations. For this reason, considering human and social factors in knowledge management makes sense. Thomas et al. (2001) point out that most KM approaches emphasize getting 'the right information to the right people at the right time' (p. 864). But how can you know what is 'right' without understanding the individual information needs and social context? Holding on to this dizzying array of meanings of knowledge management is enough to put you off balance! For the sake of expediency, let us seek a bit of 'terra firma' by settling on a definition of KM for the purposes of this book. Thus we have agreed that knowledge management is not only a 'problem of capturing, organizing, and retrieving information, but is an activity that is inextricably bound up with human cognition and in a human context' (Thomas et al., 2001: 863).

The ultimate goal of knowledge management is to 'induce professionals to mediate their tacit knowledge in a simple and concrete way, so that the right person can get access to it and use it' (Kjellin and Stenfors, 2002: 268). These authors explain that tacit knowledge is unarticulated. For this reason, one of the goals of knowledge management is to facilitate the translation of 'tacit' knowledge into 'explicit' knowledge, i.e. knowledge that resides outside of the mind or experience of one individual. Because tacit knowledge is often difficult to articulate, knowledge managers must derive techniques that encourage and facilitate the sharing of this valuable resource.

The methods used to collect 'tacit knowledge' can be either social or technical. Social methods might include interviews and focus groups. Such group dynamics encourage participants to think critically, to be reflective, and to mutually construct meaning around their work experience. The definition of knowledge management that seems to best fit within the context of design projects is that used for 'project knowledge management.'

> ... Knowledge management [*sic*] is coordinating organizational knowledge and information to enable increased project management capability and to achieve business value from that capacity. This concept elevates fundamental communications in the project management environment from mere data transfer to the conveyance of ideas, perceptions, experiences, and interpretations that transcend the simple exchange of information. (Hill, 2004: 99)

In the next section we will explore some practical steps that will guide the design team in the management of both data and knowledge in a way that will contribute to a successful project.

Managing project knowledge

Hopefully, in the preceding four chapters we have convinced you that information design is not a linear sequential activity performed best by machines. Information design demands embracing and understanding the complexities of human information seeking, information use in organizations, and organizational behavior. In the process of gathering data through the creation of information use scenarios, information designers collect data about potential users of the systems under development, as well as gain expertise and insight, and contribute to a body of 'knowledge' that might be useful to all on the project team.

> Knowledge work is not a solitary occupation, but it involves communication among loosely structured networks and communities of people. (Thomas et al., 2001: 866)

Members of an information design team must not only employ but use with regularity the tools previously agreed upon to collect and manage the data for a design project. Collecting the data generated throughout the project and storing it on individual hard drives, recording devices, and other data storage devices will only benefit the individual team member who has access to each particular device and not the group as a whole. First, the project team must consider in what file formats will the data be collected. Will there be paper, e-mail messages, web pages, or PDA files? Has the team agreed upon the use of one system to collect the content of the project? Have schedules been established for performance or technical status reports? How will such reports be submitted and archived? How will the data be organized and accessed?

While large corporations may have expensive data or content management systems and data mining tools in place, the authors suggest there are other less expensive tools and processes to put in place. Technical tools to support content management and data mining might include the use of blogs, time and task tracking, and surveys. John Carroll, in a presentation in Fall 2005 to a community of scholars at the

University of Texas at Austin, discussed a collaboration tool that not only collected all of this data (blogs, time and task tracking, reports, etc.), but could also display all the data in one single window and allow movement among the different components with ease. The tool is called BRIDGE (Basic Resources for Integrated Distributed Group Environments) and is available for anyone to download and install at *http://bridgetools.sourceforge.net/*.

Among our recommendations for managing the 'knowledge' are the following.

- Plan and implement a network accessible database to store and back up large data files (recordings, video recordings, transcripts, etc.).

- Establish and agree upon group communication systems (e-mail, online forums such as Geeklog (*http://www. geeklog.net*) or blogs). (Geeklog is a weblog powered by PHP and MySQL that allows individuals to register and submit stories or comments relevant to a particular project, as well as having the flexibility to determine and monitor short- and long-term goals for the communication and management of information/knowledge.)

- Develop an online form that interfaces with a searchable database to collect 'personnel expertise' and contact information.

- Establish a standard for subject fields and descriptors with clear, commonly understood definitions.

To rephrase a commonly used precept, 'knowledge management technologies are about delivering the right information to the right people at the right time' (Knight and Howes, 2003: 99). The project team must determine what kinds of data, information, and knowledge.

Summary

This chapter has explored the definitions, principles and tools of project and knowledge management with the goal that the application of basic project management tenets will serve as a practical guide to managing your design project as well as the 'knowledge' and expertise accrued during the project. By employing the above principles the project team will be capable of determining and monitoring the short- and long-term goals for communication and management of information and knowledge. The principles and tools discussed in this chapter will not only guide the planning, development, and management of an information design project but shape the final product by using the data gathered on information needs and context of the potential information users.

In the next chapter we will explore strategies and methods for presenting ideas that evolve during the project design process.

References

Berkman, E. (2001) 'When bad things happen to good ideas,' *Darwinmag.com*. Retrieved February 17, 2004 from: *http://www.darwinmag.com/read/040101/badthings.html*.

Ergazakis, K. et al. (2002) 'Knowledge management in enterprises: a research agenda,' in D. Karagiannis and U. Reimer (eds), *Practical Aspects of Knowledge Management*. Berlin: Springer, pp. 37–48.

Hill, G.M. (2004) *The Complete Project Management Office Handbook*. New York: Auerbauch.

Kjellin, H. and Stenfors, T. (2002) 'Process for acquiring knowledge while sharing knowledge,' in D. Karagiannis and U. Reimer (eds), *Practical Aspects of Knowledge Management*. Berlin: Springer, pp. 268–80.

Kliem, R. and Ludin, I.S. (1998) *Project Management Practitioner's Handbook*. New York: AMACOM.

Knight, T. and Howes, T. (2003) *Knowledge Management – A Blueprint for Delivery: A Programme for Mobilizing Knowledge and Building the Learning Organization*. Oxford: Butterworth Heinemann.

Koenig, M.E.D. (1999) 'Education for knowledge management,' *Information Services and Users*, 19: 17–31.

Thomas, J.C., Kellogg, W.A. and Erickson, T. (2001) 'The knowledge management puzzle: human and social factors in knowledge management,' *IBM Systems Journal*, 40 (4): 863–84.

Presentations of ideas

In Chapter 4 we discussed the importance of communications among stakeholders. In this chapter, we focus on the detailed steps for presenting ideas. The purpose of the presentation or communication of ideas is to establish a 'knowledge community' (Erickson and Kellogg, 2002).

Knowledge community

We have all had the experience of encountering misunderstandings during a communication process. Such misunderstandings can result from the complexity of expression, the usage of words, the basic background of the topic, or the lack understanding of the context. To prevent such misunderstandings, project stakeholders should be encouraged to present their ideas in ways that are natural and comfortable to them. When stakeholders and project team members can present their ideas clearly, they are also sharing valuable knowledge within a community of stakeholders. The keystones of a knowledge community include a friendly, open environment and culture, engaging activities, and meaningful expressions. Before we discuss these keystones further, let us consider a few common scenarios that exemplify the importance of a mechanism by means of which stakeholders may share their ideas.

Example 1: Supermarket shoppers

In my neighborhood supermarket the management posts shoppers' feedback on a physical bulletin board. On a form provided by the supermarket customers include comments on their shopping needs and product preferences as well as other comments on the store's shopping environment. Some shoppers even draw pictures to communicate their ideas in a graphical form. The lower half of the form includes the store manager's response. Such communications not only strengthen customer relationships but also contribute to a knowledge community. Shoppers are encouraged to share their demands (knowledge) and the supermarket managers are able to receive and react to such knowledge through the shoppers' presentations.

Example 2: Online customer reviews

It is now common for many online business establishments to provide customer reviews about their merchandise such as 'Top 10 Hot Items,' 'What Else People Buy/View,' etc. These functions can be of value to customers who are about to make an important or expensive purchase because we all want to get the best possible deal. For instance, recently I was looking to purchase a new automobile. In addition to trips to local car dealerships and auto manufacturers' websites, I read a number of online customer reviews to become more familiar with my chosen automobile. Through the reviews, I became knowledgeable about the new features and accessories provided in the vehicles under consideration. Furthermore, I gained important vocabularies about these cars. The learning experience made my purchase experience both informed and more efficient – I knew exactly what I wanted and exactly what to expect from the business transaction.

Example 3: Architecture and public opinions

In several recent architectural projects in the United States, the design teams displayed their models for the public to view and provide feedback on the plans. Two of these current projects include the plans for the new World Trade Center and the Olympic Village project, both in New York. While viewing the proposed architectural models, viewers can cast their votes and voice their opinions regarding the projects.

By means of new computational technologies, architects can generate computer-based 3D images for online presentations that include detailed constructional drawings and physical models for their clients. Such presentations can graphically convey design ideas between the design teams and their clients. Some important projects even offer clients virtual tours not only to view a model of the project but also to vividly experience movement through the proposed construction. Through such 3D models the design teams can employ perception-rich presentations to communicate with their clients and solicit from their clients feedback based on these virtual presentations.

In the above three examples we have emphasized that appropriate and varied means of presentation are critical to building channels of communication between the design team and stakeholders. Do you remember the last time you heard the question 'What do you mean by this?' in response to an idea? Often the motivation behind such a question is a misunderstood word or the lack of a graphic representation to explain an idea or concept. The question 'What do you mean by this?' illustrates the importance of planning for effective presentation and communication systems between the design team and the client. To establish effective presentation and communication systems, we must consider the following questions:

- Why do we need this particular presentation or communication system?

- What do we hope to gain from the system?

- How do we get what we want from the system?

- What can we do with the information we get from the system?

By developing such presentation and communication systems, we can establish a public forum within which knowledge is provided, shared, used, and accumulated by stakeholders. Such interactions can foster the development of a project that is grounded in the different social perspectives of its stakeholders.

Types of stakeholders

Project stakeholders will most likely all contribute some knowledge to a presentation/communication system. Since our stakeholders are varied and unique in their perspectives, preferences for communication, and conceptual orientations, we must know how to collect ideas from them. The first step in planning for a presentation/communication system is to analyze the types and levels of importance of the project stakeholders.

Internal stakeholders

Internal stakeholders include the members of the design team, company employees, etc., and comprise a more homogenous community compared to external stakeholders. Within an internal, homogenous community it should be relatively easy to share ideas using a platform that is compatible and accessible to this internal group. This is especially true when an organization has existing electronic media and transmissions systems in place.

For instance, we can assume that internal stakeholders use the same sized paper for copy machines and printers, as well as having common configurations for their computers and monitors. For this reason, copy machines or printers without any modifications can easily reproduce ideas presented on paper. Audio-visual materials can be viewed on TV or a computer monitor. Consider, for example, those incidents we have all experienced when we must spend time justifying documents to make them compatible for our particular copying or printing devices. 'Hmmm... should I reduce the size to 90 per cent? Should the document format be two pages? Should it be double-sided?' Or 'Oops, I can't open this movie file. I wonder which software it requires?' *Compatibility* is critical for presenting and sharing ideas.

Compatibility

With the increased availability of multimedia products on the Internet through web browsers we have all encountered the difficulties of compatibility. Take, for example, the use of e-mail. How often do you receive an e-mail message that arrives with all the HTML tags because your particular e-mail program is not capable of or configured to display a web-based message? Or perhaps the e-mail software you use doesn't support text enhancement feature such as underline, bold, or italics (see Figure 6.1). Prior to sending critical presentations through e-mail, it should be determined whether the recipient's e-mail program is capable of or

Figure 6.1 Different text display

```
Date: Thu, 30 Jun 2005 18:21:59 +0800
From: ???
To: ???
Subject: PAPER
Parts/Attachments:
  1   OK    ~22 lines   Text (charset: BIG5)
  2 Shown   ~41 lines   Text (charset: BIG5)
----------------------------------------

  [ The following text is in the "big5" character set. ]
  [ Your display is set for the "ISO-8859-1" character set.  ]
  [ Some characters may be displayed incorrectly. ]

¹o½g¤å²¹¥x/EŪ¨S¦³,-n¦A¤@¦¸²À·ÐSA.
ŞÚ-n±Ñ¨h¥óÀàµ¹ŞA,ŞÚ¬0«Ü§V¤0Şä¹L,
¥x/EŪ²º¹Î©ÑÀ¦³¹£¨S¦³¨åÀ¨°»òµ[¸«ô¨USAÀ¨ŞÚŞäŞä¬Ý, ÁÁÁ!
(ŞÚ¥ÎÀ¦]»Ú¦X§@¦b¥x/EŪÂà¤F§Ö¤@-Ó¤ë,¹£¨S¦³,«ô¨UÅo)
```

configured to display e-mail messages in both ASCII codes
and the HTML format. For international organizations the
use of multiple languages can present another big problem.
If you are sending important information in a language
other than English, make sure the recipient's e-mail program
is configured to display the language used.

A further situation is all too common: you can't open
attached files (see Figure 6.2). The design teams need to

Figure 6.2 Functions available at Yahoo!

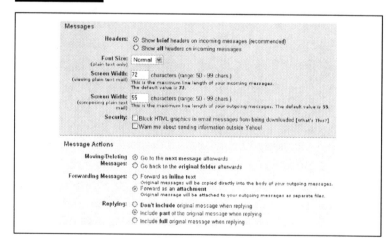

control what software programs the internal stakeholders can use to present their ideas. Common software programs must be made available to all stakeholders. The design team also needs to establish guidelines for the formats of information sharing:

- *Text* – should the design team provide a text template for the internal stakeholders?

- *Images and videos* – what file format(s) can be used for images and videos?

- *Sound and voice* – what file format(s) can be used for sound and voice?

Often it is a surprise to some that even the use of the Web is a third problematic area. Did you know that different web browsers with their different versions and various plug-ins can often cause display problems or display information in different ways? The design team must remember to specify all requirements, such as browsers, versions, monitor resolutions, and particular plug-ins to prevent difficulties with the sharing of web-based information.

External stakeholders

Unquestionably, the above considerations also are important to the external stakeholders. However, we need to pay even more attention to the collection of quality data from external stakeholders and to the sharing of the data within the design team, since the external stakeholders and their information and communication environments can be difficult to anticipate.

To obtain quality data from external stakeholders, the design team must be aware of the following:

- collectable data;
- shareable data;
- data quality.

Collectable data

When asking questions, the design team must keep the most important thing in mind, 'Are the stakeholders able to answer the questions?' External stakeholders are very different and have a wide range of characteristics, from educational level to cultural background, from language to particular knowledge, and from geographic location to neighborhood environment. These variables can hinder the design team from collecting desirable data from external stakeholders.

Are external stakeholders capable of providing useful responses to the team's questions? As we know young children may not have sophisticated writing or speaking skills, but we can still communicate with them. Non-native language speakers may have limited ability to articulate or explain ideas. People in a conservative or constrained community may not express their opinions freely. For this reason the design team must be sensitive to these situations, or the external stakeholders may not be able to or feel free to answer questions or provide information without misunderstanding.

For instance, the US federal government hired many workers to distribute materials and survey residents when conducting the 2000 Census. These workers physically visited households and explained to the respondents how to fill out the survey. For quality data collection the survey bureau hired ethnic workers whose job was to assist their fellow citizens to break down the inevitable barriers of language and culture. These strategies helped the survey bureau obtain collectable, quality data.

Shareable data

Once the design team obtains data from external stakeholders, the team needs to share the data with internal units. How will you share hard-copy surveys? How will project team members view the results of online questionnaires? What are the alternatives to downloading and manipulating raw survey data? What is the plan to collect and distribute data that includes sketches, photos, voice recordings, videotapes, and other media? The answers to these questions can contribute to planning for compatibility in data sharing which we have discussed earlier in this chapter. The team must foresee the circulation process or the data collection becomes meaningless and less useful.

Data quality

After obtaining collectable data and ensuring that the data is shareable, the team must examine the data quality. The first question is whether the data is biased, reliable, and comprehensive. An interesting phenomenon in the United States is that many television programs increasingly are using pools of viewers to determine which contestants can advance or win. While these survey methods and results are often very controversial, the TV shows remain very popular among their viewers.

The use of online voting is also popular among some news media. Readers are encouraged to cast their ballots and voice opinions on a variety of current 'hot' topics. The ratings and personal statements reflect a variety of perspectives, but the news media always caution their viewers that the rankings or ratings are not comprehensive and can be biased. So why make the ratings available at all when they might be biased? Clearly, the reasons depend on what goal the design team wants to achieve. For TV shows and news media, being controversial may help boost their sales and viewing rates. On the other hand, the design team must be cognizant that the use of online public forums and voting is only appropriate when a quality management mechanism is in place.

Appropriate technologies for stakeholders and the design team

After analyzing stakeholders internally and externally, and understanding the importance of data quality, the design team is ready to collect data. So now we discuss appropriate technologies for the team and stakeholders.

Low tech and high tech

People sometimes joke about something being 'low tech' or 'hi tech.' It is important to acknowledge that use of technology does not always guarantee positive results, and may introduce a new set of problems. The use of a particular technology should derive from a thoughtful consideration of 'the right user, the right time, and the right place.' Our options for various hi- or low-technologies are wide and varied. For this reason, the design team must be knowledgeable about the stakeholders' skills, knowledge, motivations, and time constraints.

The controversial incidents during the 2000 US presidential election in Florida underlined the importance of understanding project stakeholders' skills and knowledge regarding the use of technology. In that election, electronic voting devices were used, but due to the confusing and often misleading electronic ballot display interface numerous voters chose wrong candidates or voided their ballots after realizing their mistake. The chaotic situation had a substantial (even disconcerting) impact on the results of the Florida election.

The mistakes made by the voters were in part the result of decentralized government agencies in the US who had little expertise in creating and managing an election using e-ballots. In the US, local authorities manage the elections and each authority has different voting procedures and designs and different devices for local citizens to use. Ballots changed from paper to computer monitor, from punch card to sliding machine, and often from one language to multiple languages. There were numerous variations of new and old voting procedures. The point to be taken from this example is that voters were confused by all the different technologies in use to cast their vote, as well as by the poorly planned and tested user interfaces on the voting machines!

To avoid making the mistake outlined above, the local authority in Austin, Texas (the place these authors call home) cautiously conducted a study on voters several years prior to the actual implementation of electronic voting. Electronic voting machines were placed at a shopping mall and shoppers were encouraged to try out the machines. This pre-test had a threefold purpose:

- to understand voters' skills and their possible difficulties with the machines;
- to test the machine's functionality; and
- to publicize and visualize the new voting changes.

In this example, the skills and knowledge of the voters and the new voting machine had to be aligned so voters would be successful in casting their vote. In the meantime, by experiencing first-hand the significant changes in the system, voters had the opportunity to acquire new skills and knowledge and the changes received wider publicity. In other words, voters more or less knew what to expect in the new e-voting system.

When using technologies, stakeholders' motivations and time constraints must also be taken into account. Airport check-in kiosks, for instance, are increasingly used in the US. The airline companies expect that the kiosks will provide travelers with timely services, reduce check-in congestion, and ease their employees' workload. Personally, I like to use the kiosks to avoid the long line at the check-in counter. My primary motivator is to save time. However, some might say 'Why am I doing this? It is a waste of time! Why is it not working? I don't understand why my reservation isn't showing up. Oh well, I am not going to use it!' This would not be what you want to hear from your stakeholders. You want to motivate them and offer them immediate benefits (time savings, efficiencies, and hassle-free usage) for using a new technology.

Airline kiosks could shorten your flight check-in time. Theoretically, you can choose an available seat without going through a customer specialist to do so. The customer should feel that they are in control! Several airlines even provide online pre-check-in that allows you to print out a boarding pass so you can go directly to the departure gate. In an ideal world, these technologies should motivate travelers to use them and to save time. However, people have problems with these kiosks, and many of these are frequent travelers. On the other hand, infrequent travelers may prefer to skip the hassle of an unfamiliar kiosk and let the check-in counter staff take care of them. Moreover, the infrequent traveler may not want to spend the time becoming familiar with the kiosks. So, in anticipation of customer difficulties, airlines often station employees nearby to provide travelers with assistance. If we define the kiosks as high tech and human assistance as low tech, this use of both illustrates a popular compromise for most travelers.

From the above two examples, we can see that the appropriateness of the technologies used must be based on stakeholders' skills and knowledge as well as their motivation and time-saving. The two examples also demonstrate the differences between physical and digital devices. The design team must consider these factors when collecting data from stakeholders for system design.

Physical and digital

Anticipating the volume of data should be a major consideration for data collection regarding the use of physical and digital devices. Questionnaires exemplify the use of both physical and digital devices. Online questionnaires have become very popular and many websites offer limited features at no charge. As Schonlau, Fricker, and Elliott state, '... they are believed to be faster, better, cheaper, and easier to conduct ...' (2002: xiii). The efficiency of online surveys depends on whom you are surveying! The following are some basic considerations for online questionnaires.

Sample size

The size of the sample should be big enough for the team to invest time, personnel, and resources in conducting an online questionnaire. With online questionnaires not only do respondents have to fill out their answers but the design team also has to analyze the data, and the whole data collection and analysis process can be very technologically complicated. If the sample size is too small, the cost-effectiveness of this data collection method will be minimal or nill. So the design team must weigh up and balance the sample size and efficiencies when considering the use of digital devices.

Targeted population

I witnessed some surveyors asking travelers to answer questions at a train station during a recent trip to London. The survey focused on the service quality provided at the train station. The surveyors were not always able to find travelers willing to answer the survey. At a busy place like a train station, commuters are rushing to catch their trains and do not want to be delayed. How do we effectively recruit respondents at such a busy place? Could the survey be done digitally? If so, how? If not, what else could be done? We often see customer surveys collecting dust at business establishments. Why did customers ignore these surveys? First, many business establishments do not enforce the collection of surveys. Second, customers do not like to answer long or complicated surveys. Third, often the survey is not convenient for customers to complete because there are no pens available or there isn't a space on which they can write. The design team must understand the targeted population to determine how to use analog and digital devices separately or together, and whether human assistance is needed or not.

Tracking respondents

'I'm sorry, I would like to answer your survey but I can't find it now. Can you please send me a new copy?' This excuse is one of the challenges for questionnaire recall. When conducting surveys, the return rate is always a major issue for researchers as a reasonable return rate is required for data validity. Researchers frequently spend time tracking targeted survey respondents. When paper-based questionnaires are used, they often get lost and result in a low return. An online questionnaire can improve such a situation, as long as the respondent hasn't lost the web address. The project team can monitor the data collection by respondents' status and remind them to fill out the survey. In most cases digital devices can more effectively track respondents.

Rich survey content

Online questionnaires can include more media in the content that may assist the design team to obtain desirable feedback. For instance, an information system's features are difficult to describe by text only; however, the design team can use animations or videos to demonstrate the functions step by step. Such rich demonstrations help respondents understand the use of the information system and can provide accurate responses to the survey.

Dynamic data display

Online questionnaires also allow the design team to monitor the progress of data collection. Once the questionnaires have been answered and the data collected is in the database, the design team can review the data set to determine what steps are required next. The design team may find too many questionnaires are from the same gender, age group, geographic location, etc. Based on the purpose of the study, the design team may need to take immediate action to recruit other respondents and so avoid any imbalance in the data collected. Another challenging situation is when respondents misinterpret questions and provide incorrect answers whereas the design team needs 'quality' answers.

Paper-based questionnaires do not provide these time-efficient strategies for collecting quality data. However, these strategies should not be used to influence the procedure of data collection because they may generate biased results.

Data analysis

When the design team implements a well-planned data collection procedure using an online questionnaire, data analysis can be accomplished more effectively. First, data elements (i.e. age, gender, income category, level of satisfaction) are digitally recorded as soon as respondents answer the survey. Second, the design team can compare the data elements by a variety of means and generate appropriate visual presentations. Third, since the data set is born digitally, the design team can merge several data sets as a mega set for presenting their findings in a variety of ways. Finally, raw digital data is easier to share and analyze.

Fragile data

The design team must be aware that all data is fragile in both digital and analog formats. As we have discussed earlier regarding collectable and shareable data, the design team should look at a life cycle of ideas and be clear on how those ideas will be collected, shared, recorded, and discarded during the development of the information system. At the different stages of the life cycle, the design team must decide in what format the ideas should be presented. Ideas are constantly being transformed from one format to another during the different stages of the system development. At the beginning of the project, stakeholders may use scratch paper to explore ideas. Later on only selected ideas may be recorded and disseminated in other formats. Ideas may be presented in very different formats: as files attached to e-mail messages, as hard-copy documents in post-mail, or as downloadable files online. On the other hand, stakeholders may react to those ideas in a different format. For example, suppose I receive a survey via e-mail, print it out, answer it, and mail it back to the researcher. In this case, the survey is in a digital format but my response is in a physical format.

Since ideas are recorded in many formats, preserving the data in the whole process can be a big challenge to the design team. The design team must carefully examine the life cycle of the data and establish guidelines for its management. In Chapter 7, we will discuss the life cycle of ideas in greater detail.

Multimedia

The use of multimedia enables the design team to create settings in which stakeholders can provide true responses to the team. Multimedia refers to the variety of media that can be used. Trade shows are great places to see how companies use multimedia to catch visitors' attention. Based on their products' features, companies may employ models, artifacts, food, sound, video, etc., to give visitors concrete ideas about what their products are.

At a household trade show, for instance, we may see a kitchen equipped with start-of-the-art appliances. 'Look at this! What a lovely kitchen! The range looks very good in this setting.' The company creating the display may present more than just the appliances, but use colors, lighting, and floral arrangements to set a context for their exhibit. Its employees use the appliances to demonstrate cooking and show how the appliances fit into a variety of lifestyles. The appliances may provide visitors with some initial interest but a live demonstration and interaction with the audience establish connections between vendors and show visitors. The key here is how to use multimedia to provide stakeholders with vivid experiences.

TV shopping channels are another example of providing viewers with live demonstrations. On these channels viewers can see demos of cookware, household appliances, holiday items, cosmetics, etc., and sales people chat with customers over the phone. Such interactions are designed to motivate viewers to purchase products. Can you imagine how unconvincing shopping channels would be without live demonstrations?

Ideas are often vague and for this reason it is not enough simply to present them by means of one single medium. Furthermore, it is also difficult to exchange ideas via just one medium. The design team must maximize the use of multimedia to provide stakeholders with sensory-rich environments so they can reveal their genuine reactions and so prompt discussion.

What strategies will work?

After discussing internal and external stakeholders, the compatibility of technologies, data quality, and use of appropriate technologies, we have to pay attention to strategies for collecting stakeholders' ideas. The design team must be flexible in applying different strategies to collect those ideas.

However, there are no certain rules to guarantee that you will collect quality ideas in sufficient quantity. Combined methods should be used to reach the goals of data collection. For instance, the team may need to collect ideas first from focus group discussions and then use those ideas to construct a questionnaire. Responses from the questionnaire may also need follow-up group/individual interviews for in-depth explanation.

A combination of different methods will help the team to design better research tools, to collect more useful data, and to better understand the data. This integrated approach will also assist the design team to recognize and capture social phenomena surrounding the stakeholders regarding the use of the information system.

Summary

The purpose of the presentation or communication of ideas is to establish a 'knowledge community.' The keystones of a knowledge community include a friendly, open environment and culture, engaging activities, and meaningful expressions. When stakeholders and project team members can present their ideas clearly, they also are sharing valuable knowledge within a community of stakeholders. To establish effective presentation and communication systems, we must consider the following questions.

- Why do we need this particular presentation or communication system?
- What do we hope to gain from the system?
- How do we get what we want from the system?
- What can we do with the information we get from the system?

The design team can use different communication technologies with stakeholders. However, it must be understood that the appropriateness of the technologies used is based on the stakeholders' skills and knowledge as well as their motivation and the time-saving to be achieved. The team also needs to recognize the differences between physical and digital devices when collecting data from stakeholders for system design.

References

Erickson, T. and Kellogg, W.A. (2002) 'Social translucence: designing systems that support social process,' in J.M. Carroll (ed.), *Human–Computer Interaction in the New Millennium*. New York: ACM Press, pp. 325–45.

Schonlau, M., Fricker, R.D., and Elliott, M.N. (2002) *Conducting Research Surveys via E-Mail and the Web*. Santa Monica, CA: Rand.

7

Life cycle of ideas

Ideas are broadly defined throughout this book and evolve during the development of an information system project. At the beginning of the project, stakeholders contribute their ideas using different media; later on, ideas may be labeled by other means such as knowledge, documents, and assets. In the dynamic and fast-paced development of the project, we need to understand the important concepts of the management of knowledge, documents, and assets. In Chapter 5, we discussed the basic principles of knowledge management (KM). In this chapter, we look at the life cycle of ideas in terms of the different aspects of knowledge, documents, and assets. Ideas, knowledge, documents, and assets are critical ingredients for a successful implementation of the system project. Remember that these key terms – *ideas, knowledge, documents,* and *assets* – are not separate concepts but that they represent information at different stages of an information system project. These key terms in a life cycle and their relationships with one another need to be identified.

Ideas and knowledge

We all have different ideas about a variety of things in our lives, and we often comment on many topics and share our ideas with the people around us. In Chapter 6, we discussed the importance of a *knowledge community* in the development of an information system project. A knowledge community encourages stakeholders to contribute ideas freely. Ideas may not be fully matured in the beginning but they can serve to initiate discussion and lead to essential discoveries. During the discussion, ideas are polished by stakeholders and stakeholders become more knowledgeable in the process. In this way a new expanded knowledge is generated from discussing ideas. Original ideas, the discussion process, and modified ideas are all vital components of a knowledge community.

Once we understand the relationship between ideas and knowledge, we can see why knowledge management is part of a life cycle of ideas. In order to manage knowledge, first it is necessary to identify how stakeholders contribute and present ideas and then consider their discussion processes and modification of ideas, and the knowledge community as a whole. After analyzing these factors, strategies for managing knowledge can be developed.

Ideas and documents

Ideas may be presented in many different formats and media. However, ideas that are in recorded forms can be managed and distributed. In this book recorded ideas are identified as *documents*. Levy (2003) defines documents as 'talking things' (p. 30), which 'are things we create to take responsibility for some of our concerns' (p. 31). These things are not only text but also images and graphics, voice and sound, as well as moving images. With emerging technologies, they are created digitally, e.g. in the form of e-mail messages, word-processed documents, and voice messages on mobile phones.

Levy points out that 'the written forms provide stable reference points that help to orient us in the social space' (2003: 38). The system design team must record important ideas in the entire development process and establish policies for such practices. These policies and practices are important for legal and organizational considerations. For example, mismanagement of documentation occurred during the collapse of Enron. At that time Enron was the Number 1 energy trading company in the US, and Arthur Andersen LLP, then a leading financial consulting company, was responsible for handling Enron's financial reports. During an investigation by the US Security and Exchange Commission (SEC), Arthur Andersen's top administrators asked its employees to shred documents. As it was later revealed, such actions hindered the SEC's enquiries about Enron's accounting practices and eventually led to the demise of Andersen. The Enron-Andersen example indicates the importance of proper document management.

Document management must also consider local needs and global accessibility, especially for a large-scale information system. Local needs can range from the use of documents to the display of documents. For example:

Public Relations Department: 'We need this document in format X, to be available by next week for a town hall meeting.'

Marketing Department: 'Can we convert this figure from format A to format B?'

Graphic Design Department: 'We need to show this picture in a bigger size.'

The design team must satisfy such enquiries from stakeholders.

Global accessibility lets stakeholders retrieve documents and promotes potential sharing of ideas. Compatibility is the key to the success of global accessibility. In Chapter 6, the importance of compatibility was discussed. When stakeholders are geographically separated, the design team must consider their environmental limitations (e.g. Internet connections, bandwidth, storage facilities, system security, and software).

Ideas and assets

After ideas have been produced and discussed they become mature and are rendered into fixed formats. At this stage, ideas are called *assets*, and are the property of an organization. The attributes of assets depend on the nature of the organization and agreements between the organization and its stakeholders. For example, in general, government employees do not retain the ownership of anything created in the exercise of their jobs, such as reports, letters, or pictures. Similar principles are applied to private companies. However, there can be gray areas in individual cases. Organizations need to consult their legal departments regarding the scope of their assets.

The broadcasting, media, and publishing industries, as we describe them in this book, fostered the concept of assets. These industries produce massive amounts of new objects daily and the number has been rapidly increased by digital technologies. With such a digital boom, companies are moving from physical archiving to digital asset management. For example, in the pre-digital era, photojournalists took analog pictures and newspapers houses published the photos in their papers. Later on, the photos were archived for future use. Today, most photojournalists use digital cameras to capture pictures and the photos are eventually published in both physical (newspaper) and digital (online) formats. Often, readers can even purchase photos online. Such changes allow newspaper publishers to produce content more effectively and also to bring in more revenue.

Therefore organizations need to have long-term goals for asset management. Such goals will serve a threefold purpose: the protection of intellectual properties, revenue generation, and development of future ideas. With regard to property protection, an asset management system must be able to handle assets, their relevant documents, and legal information. With adequate asset management, companies can shorten the production time and deliver assets for the content of their products. For instance, newspapers can quickly put out a special report on a public figure who has deceased. Some leading newspapers even make multimedia materials (e.g. historical photos, films, and sound recordings) available on their websites. To achieve such timely operations, organizations need to have asset management in place.

Well-organized assets also serve to stabilize product maintenance and to facilitate the development of ideas. For example, computer programmers can review software codes and their relevant documentation while developing a new version of a piece of software. By viewing those codes and documentation, the programmers can decide whether to improve the software based on the previous version, or whether new software structure or a new programming language is needed.

Are you feeling bewildered now with this discussion of the management of ideas, knowledge, documents, and assets? Byrne (2001) points out that the lines separating these concepts have blurred. Ideas, knowledge, documents, and assets are defined by organizations as information, and often the definitions are based upon managerial purposes. Byrne (2001) offers an overview of the following categories:

Knowledge Management (KM)
The purpose of KM is to capture and distribute the knowledge held among individuals within a corporation to other co-workers and partners, according to set rules. Not surprisingly, this class of products is especially well suited to the internal needs of organizations in knowledge-oriented industries, such as tech-intensive manufacturing and professional services firms.

Document Management (DM)
Document Management products function to help companies better manage the creation and flow of documents through the help of databases and workflow engines that encapsulate metadata and business rules.

Digital Asset Management (DAM), Asset Management (AM) or Media Asset Management (MAM)
Companies whose lifeblood revolves around their digital assets – such as entertainment firms – should organize and repurpose those assets to streamline costs and enhance revenues.

The process of a life cycle of ideas not only applies to a single project, but it is also important for the entire organization. For a community project, the ideas are the common memories of the community members. By managing ideas, an organization can observe how public opinions are presented, discussed, and formed through the life cycle. On the other side, companies need to manage the lifecycle of ideas to be competitive in the business world. Companies must apply a structured approach to organize ideas and to support innovations.

Hannaford and Poyssick suggest several important steps for team management which are also applicable to idea management (1999: 101–27).

Reasons for idea management

There are two major reasons: internal training and business competition.

Internal training

How do we do things here?

Employees need to understand the organizational culture in order to be able to face possible internal conflicts and inflexibility. The organizational administration must also be aware of these difficulties. With good idea management (KM, DM, and AM), organizations can use documents and records as training materials to educate employees. Newly hired employees in particular learn from the materials to help them integrate into the organization. For example, sales personnel learn how to approach potential buyers from previous purchasing records and analyze the records to develop business plans. On the other hand, managers can review the materials to understand internal conflicts and inflexibility and to come up with solutions to resolve problems. These processes lead to the next question.

Why did we fail or succeed?

Companies rely on good idea management to learn about their successes and failures. There are four major areas of failure:

- *On-time delivery.* Successful project implementations rely on each team member delivering his or her assignments on time. Through the records that were kept the design team can review a previous project and learn what error(s) occurred at what stage(s) and who/what unit(s) was or were responsible. Before starting a project, team leaders must have a clear timeline for the project and deadlines for each stage. Reviewing previous records will assist the team members to get a sense of what they will face and help them deliver assignments on time for the project.

- *Productivity.* Through the use of records the design team also can identify which unit(s) failed to produce assigned work and experienced low performance. The design team must carefully define the meaning of 'productivity,' which varies from organization to organization. For example, productivity may mean revenue at for-profit organizations, where it may be measured by the output of each employee, e.g. the volume of product for factory workers, articles for writers, etc.

- *Employee turnover.* 'Mary would know how to do this if she were still here.' Perhaps, you may have heard something like this at work. Companies need to use idea management to maintain knowledge contributed by employees. Each employee makes unique contributions to an organization and that wisdom is accumulated over years of work. Idea management is even more important when companies have a high turnover of employees.

- *Cost saving and revenue generating.* As a result of good idea management companies can review their records to examine the cost effects of previous projects. The purpose of the review is to eliminate redundant steps and personnel, to increase organizational efficiency, and to spend the necessary budgets in all areas. On the other hand, companies can bring in more revenue through successful asset management by repurposing products. For example, film and music companies often release new versions of old movies and sound recordings, especially those enhanced by digital technologies. Another example is the auto industry's relaunching of vintage automobiles. Through asset management, companies can rediscover the value of their long-forgotten products.

Business competition

Internal investigations help organizations identify problems and improve organizational operations as well as prepare for better organizational performance. Those improvements also assist organizations in competing with their peers. There are four major areas, as follows.

Difficulty competing with other organizations

A company's survival is dependent upon ongoing bids for business deals. For example, advertising firms must present persuasive portfolios to attract marketing accounts. The portfolios often consist of customer and market analyses, business strategies, suggested media and contents to reach target customers, etc. The portfolios are the results of ideas contributed by the employees of the advertising firms. However, not all advertising firms attract business deals successfully, and when they do not, they need to examine why this is the case. Does the winning firm have better ideas? What are the differences between the ideas of the winning firm and those of the company? Idea management can help companies recognize their weaknesses and strengths as well as improve performance in their next bid.

Another example can be found in trade shows, where companies must present the best aspects of their products to attract potential buyers. We often see some company exhibits that are crowded with prospective buyers and other vendors whose displays are empty. Why are some booths more popular than others? What are they providing that is more attractive to prospective buyers? Companies must also collect ideas from their competitors to improve performance.

Client turnover

Even when a company successfully wins a bid, this is just the beginning of a long journey. Maintaining a healthy customer relationship is a big challenge. When a company is losing customers, its administration must look to its records and find out why its clients are leaving. For example, when a client calls, his or her requests should be recorded. Which employee/office is responsible for the requests and when are solutions for such requests provided? Companies must keep these records in place to maintain a high-quality customer relationship.

Quality control for ongoing evaluation and future improvement of products and services

A high-quality customer relationship is just part of the overall quality control of products and services. Companies also need to keep maintenance records of their products and services. Cars are good examples. Car dealerships not only need to get feedback from customers but also must record details for servicing and repairs. These records are then sent back to auto manufacturers for quality control. When auto manufacturers receive information about unforeseen problems, they may even issue a recall on a particular model.

ISO 9000 Standards

Certification has become an important and valuable tool in a global economy. Companies need to adopt the standards of the International Organization for Standardization (ISO) for their products and services. The purpose of the ISO 9000 Standards is to assure quality management. The ISO 9000 Standards require organizations to fulfill:

- the customer's quality requirements, and
- applicable regulatory requirements, while aiming to
- enhance customer satisfaction, and
- achieve continual improvement of its performance in pursuit of these objectives (ISO, 2005a).

The ISO 9000 Standards provide the following principles:

1. Customer focus
2. Leadership
3. Involvement of people
4. Process approach
5. System approach to management
6. Continual improvement
7. Factual approach to decision-making
8. Mutually beneficial supplier relationships (ISO 2005b).

The eight principles involve every aspect of the 'stakeholders' and their actions involving products and services. The design team must look into the above requirements and principles and incorporate them within the life cycle of ideas.

The life cycle of ideas involves the three stages of any project for an information system: pre-project preparation, during-project development, and post-project management. A variety of data is generated at these three stages as well as throughout the entire life cycle.

Pre-project preparation

Data collection and analysis

The design team must have data in its hands to establish a basis for the project. Each organization should establish policies for data collection. Improvements in systems/products/services are based on such accumulated data.

For example, statistical data can provide some basic perspectives and serve as starting points. Figures 7.1–7.3 are examples of the 2000 US Census. The census is taken every ten years as required by the US Constitution and is used to determine the number of members of the House of Representatives for each state. It is also used to help determine the allocation of government funds, to draw state legislative districts, and for other purposes. Three different data presentations are used in each of the figures: tabulated numbers, a bar chart, and a US map with different shading indicating the distribution of population in each county. Through the three different presentations, not only can citizens better comprehend the results of the 2000 US

Figure 7.1 Extract of the annual estimates of the population for the counties of Alabama

Geographic Area	Population estimates				April 1, 2000	
	July 1, 2003	July 1, 2002	July 1, 2001	July 1, 2000	Estimates base	Census
Alabama	4,500,752	4,478,896	4,466,440	4,451,601	4,447,100	4,447,100
Autauga County	46,491	45,616	44,719	43,900	43,671	43,671
Baldwin County	151,831	148,288	144,950	141,404	140,415	140,415
Barbour County	28,816	28,971	28,967	29,043	29,038	29,038
Bibb County	21,206	21,025	21,051	19,934	19,889	20,826
Blount County	54,136	53,036	52,164	51,209	51,024	51,024
Bullock County	11,339	11,325	11,414	11,615	11,626	11,714
Butler County	20,693	20,807	21,145	21,331	21,399	21,399
Calhoun County	112,012	111,387	111,160	111,340	112,249	112,249
Chambers County	35,751	36,116	36,411	36,580	36,583	36,583
Cherokee County	24,429	24,318	24,139	24,054	23,988	23,988
Chilton County	40,878	40,445	40,022	39,801	39,593	39,593
Choctaw County	15,284	15,464	15,723	15,868	15,922	15,922
Clarke County	27,487	27,552	27,735	27,839	27,867	27,867
Clay County	14,182	14,217	14,256	14,262	14,254	14,254
Cleburne County	14,675	14,560	14,293	14,171	14,123	14,123
Coffee County	44,625	44,023	43,573	43,546	43,615	43,615
Colbert County	54,531	54,616	54,906	55,023	54,984	54,984
Conecuh County	13,588	13,747	13,929	14,052	14,089	14,089
Coosa County	11,500	11,591	11,821	11,881	11,883	12,202
Covington County	36,940	36,981	37,118	37,520	37,631	37,631
Crenshaw County	13,578	13,582	13,715	13,694	13,665	13,665
Cullman County	78,270	77,897	77,676	77,571	77,483	77,483
Dale County	49,298	49,299	49,199	49,116	49,129	49,129
Dallas County	44,977	45,335	46,037	46,222	46,365	46,365
DeKalb County	66,469	65,703	65,653	64,657	64,452	64,452

Note: The April 1, 2000 Population Estimates base reflects changes to the Censeus 2000 population from the Count Question Resolution program and geographic program revisions.

Source: Population Division, US Census Bureau.

Figure 7.2 Distribution of population by county population size

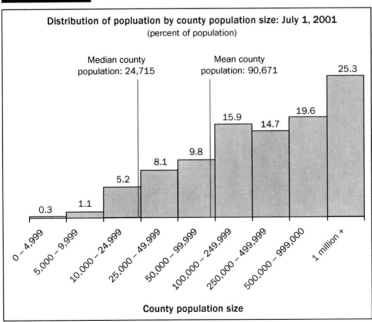

Source: US Census, 2000.

Figure 7.3 Population size for counties

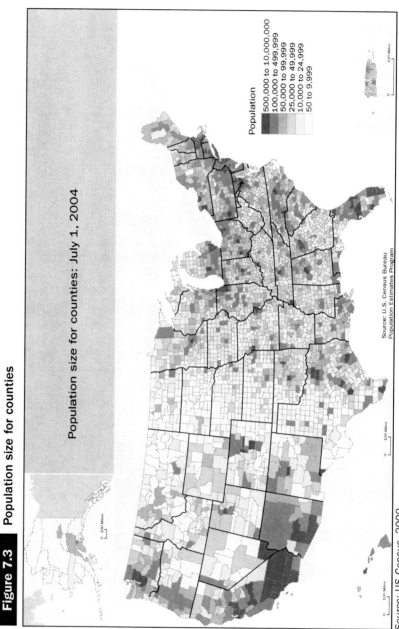

Population size for counties: July 1, 2004

Population

- 500,000 to 10,000,000
- 100,000 to 499,999
- 50,000 to 99,999
- 25,000 to 49,999
- 10,000 to 24,999
- 50 to 9,999

Source: U.S. Census Bureau
Population Estimates Program

0   100 Miles

0   100 Miles

0   100 Miles

0   100 Miles

Source: US Census, 2000.

Census but political parties and their future candidates can prepare for the next election.

With regard to data types, the design team should collect data appropriate to the particular purposes in mind, so that it is possible for the team to generate meaningful interpretations of the data for the project.

During-project development

Establish the life cycle timeline and people in charge

Time management is one of the major challenges in project development. As discussed in Chapter 4, the design team must adopt control mechanisms or tools to monitor deadlines based on time, goals, and team members.

Create simulations for stakeholders' reflection and participation

Arias et al. point out the importance of using physical and computational artifacts to help stakeholders participate in design activities (2002: 363). For example, airlines want to increase the use of self-check-in kiosks. The design team needs to conduct design activities at a real airport terminal or a terminal-like setting. Kiosks and their locations as well as different types of travelers (those of various ages, foreign tourists, non-native language speakers, adults with children, business consultants, people with special needs, etc.) are study factors. All participating users must act freely without any assistance or interruption from the design team at the setting. For example, when the participants enter the setting, they must figure out first where to go by themselves. Then they must decide whether they want to talk to people at the check-in counter or use a kiosk. When they decide to use a kiosk, their actions are observed by the design team. The design team can record what the participants do first, how soon they interact with messages from the kiosk, how often they stop, fail, or succeed, etc. With the kiosks in this particular setting, the participants can provide the design team with genuine experiences.

Record follow-up discussion

Timing is everything. It is important to know how and when to collect data from a follow-up discussion. Should a discussion take place during the design activities or after a cycle? Should the discussion be with individuals, small groups, or the entire group? People may forget what they do or why they do it after a certain period of time. On the other hand, the design team does not want to interrupt stakeholders when they are performing some tasks. Videotaping is a good idea for individuals and small groups but is not so useful for big groups or group interactions. In the above kiosk example, the design team may need to talk to the participants, but when will that be appropriate? The team must consider the entire process of data collection carefully.

Describe and access ideas

The use of a computer-aided content management system is extremely important for a large-scale project. There are many commercial systems available on the market. Before deciding which management system is appropriate, the design team must have policies for selecting, describing, and indexing ideas. Nardi suggests that scenarios should be developed 'into reusable narratives that can be cataloged and retrieved to inform a broad-based scientific approach to design' (1995: 394). By doing this, designers are able to understand the history and the previous decision-making of a target system through those narratives. Nardi also states that taxonomies are needed to manage scenarios sufficiently (1995: 395).

On the other hand, some researchers and professionals suggest that knowledge management should also focus on human experts as well (Ackerman, Pipek, and Wulf, 2003). Human experts contribute ideas, conduct design activities, and make decisions during the development of an information system. These activities should be recorded and linked to the experts. Organizations should value their internal experts and include external experts in knowledge management. Human expert-based knowledge management promotes the sharing of expertise and organizational learning. Ackerman and his colleagues believe that organizations will be benefited by such an approach. When recording ideas in the management system, the names of the contributors also should be included.

Once these practices are in place, the design team should have better ideas about which management system is suitable. The system can also be used for document/asset management in post-project management.

Post-project management

Document/asset management

Once the information system is finished, the design team can finalise all the ideas; most ideas should be in fixed formats, which means that the ideas are presented and recorded in either physical or digital media. Due to the complexity of the media formats, the design team needs to decide which are to be used before the beginning of the project to avoid problems in post-project document/asset management. These issues have been discussed in Chapter 6.

As noted above, Nardi (1995) suggests using narratives to record scenarios, which helps to reduce the massive amount of ideas to be managed and also makes scenarios more usable for future projects. The design team must decide how to record the ideas, how to preserve key examples, and how to link physical and digital media together when both formats are used. For example, should paper-based documents be digitized and available online? This consideration is related to the structure of an organization. For geographically diverse organizations, digitization is necessary for access. Meanwhile, the same considerations should be applied to other analog materials as well.

Another important issue concerning document/asset management is that the management system should support as many departments as possible in the same organization or the system will be less useful. For instance, marketing people can pull out data for customers' feedback on products/ services, usability engineers can find data from user testing, and sales personnel can use the system to retrieve media assets.

In order to ensure the flow and quality of ideas, the design team must first examine the nature and definition of ideas for the organization and for the stakeholders. Clear definitions will assist the team in developing appropriate policies and choosing a system to manage the ideas. Organizations will become more competitive and benefit by such practices. These practices also need to be integrated into the three stages of system development with consideration for supporting departmental functions within the organization.

Summary

Ideas, knowledge, documents, and assets are critical ingredients for the successful implementation of a system project. They are not separate from each other and represent information at different stages of an information system project. These key terms in a life cycle and their relationships with one another need to be identified for system design and development. Internal training and business competition are the reasons behind idea management. In order to ensure the flow and quality of ideas, the design team must first examine the nature and definition of ideas for the organization and for the stakeholders. Clear definitions will assist the team in developing appropriate policies and choosing a system to manage ideas. Organizations will become more competitive and benefit by such practices. These practices also need to be integrated into the three stages of system development with consideration for supporting departmental functions within the organization.

References

Ackerman, M.S., Pipek, V., and Wulf, V. (eds) (2003) *Sharing Expertise: Beyond Knowledge Management.* Cambridge, MA: MIT Press.

Arias, E., Eden, H., Fischer, G., Gorman, A., and Scharff, E. (2002) 'Transcending the individual human mind: creating shared understanding through collaborative design,' in J.M. Carroll (ed.), *Human–Computer Interaction in the New Millenium.* New York: ACM Press, pp. 347–72

Byrne, T. (2001) 'CM vs DM vs KM vs DAM vs SCM vs DRM – which one is right for you.' Retrieved January 7,

2005, from: *http://www.cmswatch.com/Features/ OpinionWatch/FeaturedOpinion/?feature_id=53.*

Hannaford, S. and Poyssick, G. (1999) *Teams and the Graphics Arts Service Provider.* Upper Saddle River, NJ: Prentice Hall PTR.

International Organization for Standardization (ISO) (2005a) 'ISO 9000 and ISO 14000 – in brief.' Retrieved February 20, 2005, from: *http://www.iso.org/iso/en/ iso9000-14000/index.html.*

International Organization for Standardization (ISO) (2005b) 'Quality management principles.' Retrieved February 20, 2005, from: *http://www.iso.org/iso/en/ iso9000-14000/iso9000/qmp.html.*

Levy, D.M. (2003) 'Documents and libraries: a sociotechnical perspective,' in A.P. Bishop, N.A. Van House, and B.P. Buttenfield (eds), *Digital Library Use: Social Practice in Design and Evaluation.* Cambridge, MA: MIT Press, pp. 25–42.

Nardi, A.B. (1995) 'Some reflections on scenarios,' in J.M. Carroll (ed.), *Scenario-Based Design: Envisioning Work and Technology in System Development.* New York: John Wiley & Sons, pp. 387–99.

US Census Bureau. 'Annual estimates of the population for counties of Alabama.' Retrieved March 15, 2005, from: *http://www.census.gov/popest/counties/tables/ CO-EST2003-01-01.pdf.*

US Census Bureau. 'Distribution of population by county population size.' Retrieved March 15, 2005, from: *http:// www.census.gov/popest/gallery/graphs/CO-distpop.html.*

US Census Bureau. 'Population size for counties.' Retrieved March 15, 2005, from: *http://www.census.gov/popest/ gallery/maps/popsize_c3.html.*

8

Documentation and prototyping

The focus of this chapter is on approaches to and methods of documentation and prototyping for system development. Thus far we have explored many facets of the information design process. Hopefully, the reader understands by now that information design is much more than a technical exercise, but is also very much a social process that systematically involves potential users of the information system. Previous discussion in this book notes that the development of scenarios requires the project team to routinely go back to project stakeholders for feedback and evaluation. Thus communication among members of the project team and the project stakeholders is of the utmost importance. In this chapter we will explore communicating through the development of prototypes, the role of system prototypes in the information design process, and the importance of prototype development to the communication process. The development of prototypes does much to prevent expensive, time-consuming, and frustrating problems with the use of a system product. Such problems can not only damage a project group's reputation, but may also do harm to the trust between the system user and the system developers. A University of Texas colleague who is also an experienced system developer mused that in today's information design world, 'Instead of design, test, and implement, it has become prototype, review, and redo.'

After studying stakeholders, the design team needs to produce documents from the results of its stakeholder studies for system prototyping and implementation. The prototypes will then be tested by stakeholders again (see Figure 8.1).

The use of a variety of methods for collecting data on stakeholders' behaviors and expectations with regard to the target system (an existing system or a new one) have been discussed in previous chapters. It is essential for the design team to record and 'translate' the results of the stakeholder studies into notions for system prototyping and implementation. Rosson and Carroll state that 'a user interaction scenario describes an instance of the system in use that refers to specific persons, objects, and behaviors in the world, rather than to types of users or to users' roles' (2001: 42). Based on the descriptions of user interaction scenarios, the system design team develops 'conceptual-core models'

Figure 8.1   Cycle of system development

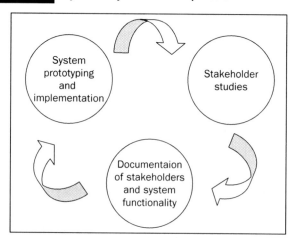

(2001: 43). Furthermore, Rosson and Carroll suggest that a 'scenario-based object model is developed for each scenario through object-oriented walkthroughs in which software objects are identified and analyzed for their roles in the scenario' (2001: 43). Through such elaborations, narratives of stakeholder studies are identified as computational objects and modules (documentation), and the system functionalities are then created based on the objects and modules (system prototyping and implementation).

What is a prototype?

According to the *Oxford English Dictionary*, a prototype is, 'The first or primary type of anything; the original (thing or person) of which another is a copy, imitation, representation, or derivative, or to which it conforms or is required to conform; a pattern, model, standard, exemplar, archetype' (OED Online). A prototype enables project designers to represent on a smaller scale the physical interactions and workings of the product. The product representation can then be evaluated by stakeholders and by the project team.

Bryan-Kinns and Hamilton (2002) discuss the dimensionality of prototypes. Their prototype dimensions include:

- The *fidelity* of the prototype ranging from low fidelity (e.g. hand-drawn sketches on paper) to high fidelity (e.g. fully interactive computer-based representations embodying both aesthetics and interaction).

- The *target audience* ranging in terms of organizational position from usability engineers ... to external participants such as clients.

- *Stage of development* at which the prototype is used. This ranges from requirements analysis through to testing ... (p. 93)

Other dimensions or traits of a prototype that should be considered include the 'accessibility and roughness' of the prototype (Erickson, 1995). Some settings such as engineering for medical purposes require more elaborate prototypes to aid surgeons and diagnosticians in analysis for therapeutic reasons. Our discussion of prototypes offers simpler, more affordable prototyping alternatives than the expensive rapid prototype models (RP) required for medical purposes.

Setting standards for prototyping

Project cost is always foremost on the mind of the project manager. For this reason the format and form of the prototype employed may be directly correlated to project funding. This is not to say, however, that a useful prototype need be expensive. A prototype (also referred to as a wireframe) for a website need not contain all of the content proposed for the site, but should at a minimum consider the layout of the home page, navigation, as well as style considerations such as font, style, and color (all easily incorporated into a style manual for cascading style sheets (CSS)). A web prototype can also include the beginnings of the information architecture. Information architecture is an umbrella term that includes usability and human–computer interaction (HCI or CHI). The term is still under debate and means different things to different people. Richard Saul Wurman describes information architecture as making things make sense and finding out what people want out of something. Information architects ask questions such as: 'What do they want to do?' 'How can we design the best design for people to do it?' and 'What is the best way for people to get what they want from an information space.' Information architecture comprises not just the 'cosmetics' of a site, but aims to achieve the right presentation as the design helps people to navigate through the information, and aims to organize information for best understanding and meaning. Rosenfeld and Morville (1998) describe information architecture as clarifying the mission and vision of an information space. It requires the developer to determine the content and functionality, as well as specifies the site organization, navigation, labeling, and searching systems. Additionally, information architecture maps out how the site will accommodate change and growth over time.

Prototyping is an important step in the development of computational objects and system functions that match stakeholders' expectations and facilitate the performance of predetermined tasks. The design team uses different approaches to execute prototyping steps based on the system structure. Artim states that there are two approaches to design descriptions: 'The first description consists of a set of use cases and scenarios that provide a structured description of examples of the domain activity to be supported ... the second description is an analysis object model that simplifies and summarizes the specification by the example provided in the scenario' (2001: 119). However, he points out that the two approaches are 'interdependent' and determined by the nature of the system and the stakeholders involved. Therefore the design team must establish the structure of the system based on studying the stakeholders and documenting observations as well as developing computational objects and modules. Artim suggests that:

A system structure consists of four important parts:

1. A partitioning of the system into its constituent parts
2. A set of rules governing the interfaces between partitions in a system
3. A set of rules governing the content of each partition within the system
4. A set of guidelines concerning the methods and descriptions used to construct the system. (2001: 121)

Documentation of stakeholder studies and system development

In order to create useful documents, we need to understand the key concepts in object-oriented documentation as defined by Wirfs-Brocks and McKean:

- An application = a set of interacting objects
- An object = an implementation of one or more roles
- A role = a set of related responsibilities
- A responsibility = an obligation to perform a task or know information
- A contract = an agreement outlining the term of collaboration. (2002: 3)

Let's use these key concepts in a common, real-world story: a bank customer is withdrawing money from an ATM machine. An application consists of the customer, the ATM machine, and the connected bank network. There are at least three objects in this case – the customer, the ATM machine, and the network – and each of them has different roles and responsibilities. The ATM machine has several roles and responsibilities since it has to provide different information and tasks to meet the customer's enquiries, which can range from withdrawing money to checking account balances and transferring funds within different accounts. The keypad and buttons of the ATM are also objects and roles. The customer uses the keypad to input account numbers, passwords, amount of money, etc., as well as to select different services. The objects need to collaborate together so the customer can successfully withdraw money from the ATM machine and receive a receipt as evidence of a contract at the end of the transaction. The use of these key concepts – *application, object, role, responsibility*, and *contract* – helps the design team to describe and structure user interaction scenarios. Clearly defined user interaction scenarios outline computational objects and modules and foster the development of the system.

The design team should also keep the descriptions of scenarios in different formats for system development, as well as apply the key concepts noted above in the descriptions of user interaction scenarios. Rosson and Carroll (2001: 46–59) use several formats to describe scenarios within the development of the system (see Table 8.1).

Table 8.1 Forms for scenario-based design

A. Initial scenario gathering	
User concern (user's actions)	Thumbnail scenario
B. High-level scenarios with brief POV scenarios	
Scenario object (different objects involved)	Point-of-view scenarios (objects' responsibilities and behaviors)
C. Design trade-offs in light of POV analysis	
Scenario feature (system functions)	Possible upside (+) and downside (−) of scenario feature

Source: Rosson and Carroll (2001).

In initial scenario gathering, the design team needs to capture stakeholders' actions in performing different tasks. In the above ATM case, for example, the customer first needs to find an ATM machine (finding an ATM); then to identify whether the ATM machine belongs to his or her bank and any possible charges (using the ATM or not); and then to decide how to withdraw money from the ATM (interacting with the ATM) (Table 8.1: A). These are some basic scenarios to start with though the scenarios can become complicated with more stakeholders with different demands, in which the design team has to develop 'point-of-view (POV) scenarios' (Rosson and Carroll, 2001). The POV scenarios are based on different perspectives of stakeholders. For instance, I have seen some ATM machines inside banks with a phone which provides bank customers with human assistance in case of difficulties and emergency. We consider those ATM machines as a POV consideration. Why? Some customers may want to talk to a bank employee when having problems with an ATM machine since not everyone is willing or able to spend his or her own time and energy sorting things out when difficulties occur (see Table 8.1: B).

In reality, most ATM machines can perform simple tasks adequately. However, they may not deal with unexpected situations well. Once I tried to withdraw money from an ATM machine but it had some mechanical problems and did not dispense the money correctly. I gave up after several attempts. The ATM machine was right next to my bank so I walked inside and talked to a customer service representative. She quickly checked my account and assured me that no money had been drawn from my account. In the meantime, she informed another office to repair the ATM machine while I used another ATM machine to get my money. I was lucky in this story. What would have happened if I wasn't near my bank or in a strange city? It might take several hours or days to resolve the whole situation. On the other hand, if the ATM machine had a phone, I could just use the phone for help.

These design considerations are then the subject of trade-offs against the POV analyses. Is a bank willing to spend the money equipping its ATM machines with a phone, or to have staff on duty either around the clock or for a limited of time? The design team has to wrestle with these considerations within personnel, budget, and system constraints (see Table 8.1: C).

The number of scenario descriptions can be enormous. However, Rosson and Carroll have developed a scenario browser to manage the descriptions effectively (2001: 64–5). This hypertext tool can be used to create, edit, and manage a set of user interaction scenarios and the analyses of POVs and design claims. The main purpose of the tool is to maintain the consistency of the scenarios and to link associated objects, collaborations, and POV analyses. The tool is also important for validating and tracking design decisions during the system implementation.

After successfully recording the observations of user interaction scenarios, the design team has to develop computational objects and modules based on the descriptions of the scenarios. Unified Modeling Language™ (UML) is a standard used to develop system applications. The benefits of using UML are the creation of a clearly defined system structure and the establishment of a library of reuseable system components and models which enable application designers to develop a new system or maintain an existing system under the pressure of time (OMG, 2005). A well-defined system structure using UML also assures its future maintenance and development. Systems designers can use UML to match the scenario descriptions, to visualize those text-based descriptions into computational diagrams, and to modularize the components and functions of the system. UML has 12 standard diagrams for the application development:

- Structural diagrams:
  - Class diagram
  - Object diagram
  - Component diagram
  - Deployment diagram
- Behavior diagrams:
  - User case diagram
  - Sequence diagram
  - Activity diagram
  - Collaboration diagram
  - Statechart diagram
- Model management diagrams:
  - Package diagram
  - Subsystem diagram
  - Model diagram.

However, use of the 12 diagrams depends on the scale and nature of the application and the support available to the system design team.

There are many UML-based tools available on the market and application designers can select a tool based on their needs (see Figure 8.2). A suggested set of selection criteria includes: repository support, round-trip engineering, HTML documentation, full UML support, pick lists, data modeling, versioning, model navigation, printing support, diagram

Figure 8.2 Choosing a UML modeling tool

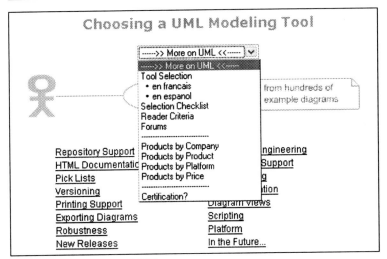

Source: Object by Design (2005).

views, exporting diagrams, scripting, robustness, platform, etc. (Object by Design, 2005).

The design team not only creates the above system documentation through the entire system development, but also prepares user documentation. The team observes stakeholders' interactions with an existing system and has an understanding of stakeholders' expectations of a new system. The results of stakeholder studies on an existing system can lead to the improvement of a new version or the design of a brand new system. They can also provide important ideas on user training and assistance. Within the different phases of the system development, the team is responsible for minimizing the frequency of errors caused either by users or by the system and for reducing the amount of learning effort required of the users. In spite of this, we have seen user's manuals and training materials from software programs or systems running to several hundred pages. However, user documentation is essential to the success of a system and it should be maintained from the beginning of the system development.

Dennis and Wixom point out three types of user documentation: reference documents, procedure manuals, and tutorials (2000: 419). They define reference documents as descriptions of system functions, procedure documents as step-by-step instructions on particular tasks, and tutorials as detailed sequences of components of the system. Reference documents clearly describe each command and function and point users to relevant commands.

With regard to procedure documents, the design team should include text and graphics, and pair text descriptions with the graphic counterparts. In the descriptions of procedures, each procedure should be broken down to a single action at a time. Multiple actions at the same time often confuse users. A number or a bullet point should label each action. Graphic presentations should be indicated in the corresponding text and close to it.

A tutorial should start with an overview which gives users a clear idea of the learning scope. The design team should limit the length and components of a tutorial based on user characteristics. Users often fail to learn from complicated and long tutorials. A tutorial also should have a review or exercise at a certain point to ensure users have learned the necessary points.

Approaches to prototyping in system design

Once all necessary documents are ready, the design team can start system prototyping. Artim points out that design visualization is important to effectively communicate with users. He suggests using screenshots of primary views of a system and cross-referencing those screenshots while prototyping (2001: 149). For reasons of effective communication, the design team must maximize the use of visual presentations in the design cycle. By doing this, the team can accelerate the processing time. However, due to the nature of the system and other environmental considerations (i.e. personnel, budget, location), Snyder suggests paper prototyping for the efficient development of a variety of systems.

> Paper prototyping is a variation of usability testing where representative users perform realistic tasks by interacting with a paper version of the interface that is manipulated by a person 'playing computer,' who doesn't explain how the interface is intended to work. (2001: 4)

According to Snyder, the benefits of paper prototyping are that it:

- provides concrete user feedback in the early stages of system development;
- enables the rapid development and testing of iterative ideas;
- provides effective communication between the design team and stakeholders;
- involves stakeholders in an environment where minimum skill is required; and
- fosters stakeholders' creativity in such an environment (p. 12).

The first step in prototyping is to create storyboards from user and system documentation. Storyboards are rough sketches/pictures of possible users' actions. Figure 8.3 shows detailed examples of withdrawing money from an ATM machine.

In the ATM case, we used Rosson and Carroll's 'Initial Scenario Gathering' method for the task analysis and then used the analysis to create the corresponding storyboards. However, the design team can use other methods for task analysis. Developing storyboards from the initial scenarios helps the design team stay on the track of system development and ensures that the storyboards will be aligned with users' expectations. After iterating the first round of

Figure 8.3 From initial scenarios to storyboards

Initial scenario gathering (withdraw money from an ATM machine)		Storyboards
User concern 1: Finding an ATM	Thumbnail scenario 1 (Text description)	
User concern 2: Identifying an ATM	Thumbnail scenario 2 (Text description)	
User concern 3: Insert a bank/ credit card	Thumbnail scenario 3 (Text description)	
User concern 4: Type password	Thumbnail scenario 4 (Text description)	
...	...	
User concern N: Receive a receipt	Thumbnail scenario N (Text description)	

storyboarding, the design team can develop more detailed storyboards based on the availability of the stakeholders. Under some circumstances, the design team may not be able to access the stakeholders. If so, the design team must have detailed user documentation right from the beginning of system development. However, wherever possible the team should constantly involve stakeholders in prototyping.

The initial scenario gathering provides an overall structure for the system. The next step is more complicated. The direction the system design takes can be either basic or comprehensive depending on the nature of the system (i.e. whether it is a new system or improvements to an existing system) and the system development plan. The basic approach focuses on minimum functionality or ongoing system maintenance. The comprehensive approach involves a 'wish list' of all the possible functions that the stakeholders would like to have in the system. At this stage, the design team should explore all possibilities to identify all functions and put each function on an index card for the next step (see Figure 8.4).

Figure 8.4 System functions on index cards

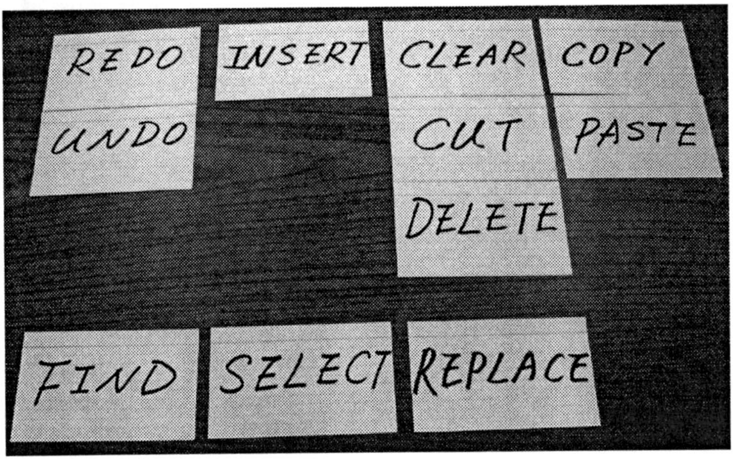

Once the functions have been described on index cards, the design team sorts the cards to prioritize the components/modules of the system and to classify relevant system functions. It may not be possible to develop all the functions at the same time with the available budget, personnel, and timeframe or other constraints. By using such a card sorting technique, the team is able to identify a feasible system development from a long-term perspective. Meanwhile, the team can use the card sorting method to categorize system functions such as basic/advanced/customized, must have/should have, etc. The method also assists the team in organizing system functions from a stakeholder-oriented approach. Looking for functions is commonly a frustrating experience for many stakeholders because the organization of functions does not always make sense to them. We frequently spend lots of time looking through the command menus of a software program or the directory of a website and trying to find the location of a particular function. Figure 8.5 presents examples of different types of system commands and web page links.

The cause of the confusion may be the name of the function or its icon, the names of the categories, or the structure of the function menu/directory. To solve these problems, the design team must work with different stakeholders to verify the names and icons of the functions and categories, the logic of the classification, and the cross-reference assistance. The card-sorting process may need several rounds to reach a stage of compromise while also performing usability testing in the organization of the system functions.

The next step in prototyping is to establish the structure of the system functions. A walk-through method should be applied to test the structure. After verifying the feasibility of the desirable functions, the design team should have a rough

Figure 8.5 Examples of system functions

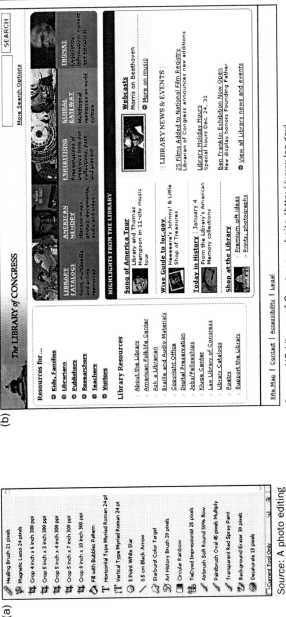

(a)

Healing Brush 21 pixels
Magnetic Lasso 24 pixels
Crop 4 inch x 6 inch 300 ppi
Crop 5 inch x 3 inch 300 ppi
Crop 5 inch x 4 inch 300 ppi
Crop 5 inch x 7 inch 300 ppi
Crop 8 inch x 10 inch 300 ppi
Fill with Bubbles Pattern
Horizontal Type Myriad Roman 24 pt
Vertical Type Myriad Roman 24 pt
5 Point White Star
0.5 cm Black Arrow
Starburst Color Target
Art History Brush 20 pixels
Circular Rainbow
TieDyed Impressionist 25 pixels
Airbrush Soft Round 50% flow
Paintbrush Oval 45 pixels Multiply
Transparent Red Spray Paint
Background Eraser 30 pixels
Desaturate 13 pixels

Current Tool Only

Source: A photo editing
tool in Adobe PhotoShop.

(b)

The LIBRARY of CONGRESS

More Search Options   SEARCH

Resources for ...

- Kids, Families
- Librarians
- Publishers
- Researchers
- Teachers
- Visitors

Library Resources

- About the Library
- American Folklife Center
- Ask a Librarian
- Braille and Audio Materials
- Copyright Office
- Digital Preservation
- Jobs/Fellowships
- Kluge Center
- Law Library of Congress
- Library Catalogs
- Poetry
- Support the Library

LIBRARY CATALOGS
Find multimedia and online resources

AMERICAN MEMORY
Historic maps, photos, documents, audio and video

EXHIBITIONS
Presentations of treasures from our collections, past and present

GLOBAL GATEWAY
Multilingual resources on world culture

THOMAS
Legislative information, current and historical

HIGHLIGHTS FROM THE LIBRARY

Song of America Tour
Library and Thomas Hampson in 11-city music tour

Wise Guide to loc.gov
Heeeeere's Johnny! & Little Shop of Treasures

Today in History : January 4
From the Library's American Memory collections

Shop at the Library
> Premium gift ideas
> Prints, photographs

Webcasts
Morris on Beethoven
> More on music

:: LIBRARY NEWS & EVENTS ::

25 Films Added to National Film Registry
Librarian of Congress announces new additions

Library Holiday Hours
Special hours Dec. 24, 31

Ben Franklin Exhibition Now Open
New display honors Founding Father

> View all Library news and events

Site Map | Contact | Accessibility | Legal

Source: US Library of Congress website (*http://www.loc.gov*).

(c)

The New York Times - Breaking News, World News & Multimedia - Mozilla Firefox

File   Edit   View   Go   Bookmarks   Tools   Help

http://nytimes.com/   Go

Getting Started   Latest Headlines   Terms of Use

Source: Command bar for Firefox, a web browser.

outline of the categories. Figure 8.6 is an example of an airline's website. There are four first-tier categories and the functions are organized in three tiers. The design team must consider the following questions regarding the walk-through process:

- How many first-tier categories should be presented?
- How many tiers should be used?
- How will the name of the categories/functions be chosen and how will they be spaced and located?

In the walk-through procedure, stakeholders are asked to perform their regular tasks using the outline of commands/functions, and see whether they can finish those tasks smoothly or not. The team can measure the outline of categories by the time taken to perform tasks, error rates and types, stakeholders' feedback, etc. The card sorting

Figure 8.6 Categories of system functions

A. Main menu bar

Reservations Center ▾   Travel Tools ▾   Promotions & Products ▾   WorldPerks ▾

B. Pull-down display

Reservations Center ▾   Travel Tools ▾   Promotions & Products ▾   WorldPerks ▾

Flight Check-In ▸
Flight Status & Timetables ▸
Luggage Information ▸   General Information
Traveler Services ▸   Luggage Check Options
Transporting Pets & Animals ▸ Carry-on Luggage
In-Flight ▸   Checked Luggage
Travel Tips   Special Luggage Items
Destination Info & Maps ▸   Restricted/Hazardous
Wireless Tools ▸   Items
                             Delayed/Damaged
                             Luggage
                             Luggage Tracking
                             Luggage Delivery
                             Services

Source: Northwest Airlines (2005).

method also allows the team to easily rearrange the structure of the categories to test stakeholders.

From the above steps, the design team will collect important data about the display of the selected functions. 'Display' here has several meanings:

- *The overall look of the system.* The stakeholders should be able to understand what the system can provide by the appearance of the display of categories. The stakeholder should not have to spend too much time looking around and learning about the system.

- *An indication of the starting point of tasks.* It should be clear to stakeholders where to start their tasks. In the airline example, it should be clear to stakeholders where to start booking a ticket.

- *The procedure for the tasks.* The relevant functions should be either grouped together or close to each other; otherwise, the stakeholders will have to memorize the locations of the related commands or look for them.

- *Recognition and identification of functions.* The stakeholders should easily be able to find and understand the command(s) they are looking for regardless of their presentation. We often have to guess the meaning of a command and use it with some doubt.

- *Use of text or graphics or both.* The design team must balance the use of text and graphics for commands. In most cases, the space for system functions and commands is limited. Explicating the meanings of the commands/functions in a limited space is a great challenge to the team. In some systems the stakeholders see a help balloon when the cursor is over the icon for a command which may help reduce the level of confusion. Other techniques are possible for the same purpose. However, the design team must pay attention to stakeholders with special needs and cultural differences regarding the use of text and graphics. This is even more important for web-based systems providing open access. In 1998, the US Congress amended the Rehabilitation Act to require federal agencies to make their electronic and information technology accessible to people with disabilities, and to eliminate barriers when developing, procuring, maintaining, or using electronic and information technology (Section 508, 2005). Some states also have similar laws for state agencies and higher education institutions.

Another important concern is the language used. Many systems provide versions in multiple languages; however, some systems do not keep the same information in all language versions due to translation difficulties, personnel, time, etc.

- *Alphabetical arrangement of categories/functions.* The order of functions and categories should be based on frequency of use and relevance to others. The design team needs to test the order with different stakeholders or allow stakeholders to customize the order.

Summary

In this discussion of 'prototyping and documentation' we have explored approaches to and methods of creating prototypes and documenting the system development process. The methods that can be applied at this stage of system development have been defined and supported by numerous examples. At this point, the reader has been introduced to the entire process of creating scenarios for information design.

The following chapter will summarize the foregoing as well as provide a useful outline of all the steps required to understand the information design process.

References

Ackerman, M.S. (2002) 'The intellectual challenge of CSCW: the gap between social requirements and technical feasibility,' in J.M. Carroll (ed.), *Human–Computer Interaction in the New Millennium.* New York: ACM Press, pp. 303–24.

Artim, J.M. (2001) 'Entity, task, and presenter classification in user interface architecture,' in M. van Harmelen (ed.), *Object Modeling and User Interface Design.* Boston, MA: Addison-Wesley, pp. 115–58.

Bryan-Kinns, N. and Hamilton, F. (2002) 'One for all and all for one? Case studies of using prototypes in commercial projects,' *NordiCHI*, October 19–23: 91–100.

Dennis, A. and Wixom, B.H. (2000) *Systems Analysis and Design.* New York: John Wiley & Sons.

Erickson, T. (1995) 'Notes on design practice: stories and prototypes as catalysts for communication,' in J.M. Carroll (ed.), *Scenario-Based Design: Envision Work and Technology in System Development.* New York: John Wiley & Sons, pp. 37–58.

Northwest Airlines. Retrieved September 19, 2005, from: *http://nwa.com.*

Object by Design. 'Choosing a UML Modeling Tool.' Retrieved September 19, 2005, from: *http://www.objectsbydesign.com/tools/modelingtools.html.*

Object Management Group (OMG). Retrieved September 19, 2005, from: *http//www.uml.org.*

Oxford English Dictionary (OED Online) (1989) 2nd edn. Retrieved September 19, 2005.

Rosenfeld, L. and Morville, P. (1998) *Information Architecture for the World Wide Web*. Cambridge, UK and Sebastopol, CA: O'Reilly.

Rosson, M.B. and Carroll, J.M. (2001) 'Scenarios, objects, and points of view in user interface design,' in M. van Harmelen (ed.), *Object Modeling and User Interface Design*. Boston, MA: Addison-Wesley, pp. 36–69.

Snyder, C. (2003) *Paper Prototyping: The Fast and Easy Way to Design and Refine User Interfaces*. Amsterdam: Morgan Kaufmann.

Wirfs-Brock, R. and McKean, A. (2003) *Object Design: Roles, Responsibilities, and Collaborations*. Boston, MA: Addison-Wesley.

9

Scenarios and information design: a summary

For the past eight chapters the authors have taken you through an exploration of a variety of theoretical, analytical, and practical methods to inform and guide your information design project. The user-focused information design process discussed in the preceding chapters has addressed the many challenges we all face in both our physical and electronic information worlds. Our goal was to provide you with a framework for the information design process that creates information spaces where use of and interaction with information is practical, useful, and perhaps even pleasant! As information users, we interact with information and information systems in a wide variety of environments, and our actions depend upon meaningful feedback from information systems. Because interaction between people and information systems is so very individualized and complicated, the creation and use of scenarios about client organizations provides information designers with new ways to better understand and plan for such interactions.

Practical theories

In Part 1 Practical Theories (Chapters 2 and 3), the reader discovered that scenarios really are just stories. For this reason information designers must be good storytellers who can create richly described scenarios to better understand the people who will be using the system and the context within which an information system is being used. Through a thoughtfully developed scenario the designer can enrich the information design plan.

To create scenarios, the information designer must first identify the primary user group(s) of the information system. By doing so information designers lay a sound foundation for the creation of the information system and establish solid, realistic goals for the system. Once the primary information system user-group is identified, the project team begins to collect data on their potential user-group. The collection of data to better 'read' the culture and functionality of an organization can begin using a wide variety of data collection strategies.

The task of exploring the client organization from both an ecological approach as well as a cognitive approach provides information designers with access to how the organization operates and what the types of users are and their information and production needs as they relate to the information system. The use of the above research methods allows the design team to get closer to the actual work practices of the client organization. More importantly the exercise of gathering this type of data will provide important contextual information that will direct the creation of the final product. Among the data collection strategies are:

- participant observation;
- administration of surveys or well-conceived questionnaires;
- one-on-one interviews;
- focus groups;

- collection of organizational artifacts;
- preparation of case studies.

Once a rich assortment of data has been collected to 'inform' the design project, the project team must construct a robust and varied system for communication among project team members as well as the project stakeholders.

Throughout the life of the information design project communication among all the stakeholders is critical to its success. In Chapter 4 strategies for planning a sound, usable communication network can do much to prevent missteps and design errors. Early in the project the design team must identify with whom they should communicate. The team must agree upon methods and forums to keep those people informed. The project team must also determine what kind of usable space must be constructed for project interaction and feedback. A well-conceived communication network provides each team member with user data to perform his or her duties. The distribution of communication through such a network accumulates *wisdom* from all stakeholders, who have the *power* to share their experience and knowledge.

Among the design team's options for an efficient and sufficient communication system is the following:

1. Create a mail list of the stakeholders.
2. Describe how to select a meaningful subject line for your e-mail message.
3. Make the content short and precise.
4. Use the Web as part of your multimedia presentation and you can avoid a wordy description in the content.
5. List all required actions.
6. Set deadlines for a reply.

Additionally, popular online tools such as blogs, wikis, and other group communication and content management systems can support ongoing efforts at communication. The appropriate use of these and other communication tools will facilitate quicker communication with stakeholders and easier collection of answers.

Theoretical practices

Throughout Part 2 of the book readers explore the Theoretical Practices for using scenarios for information design. In Chapter 5 the discussion targets strategies to manage project operations and project knowledge. Such strategies include the management of people, resources, and the project itself, as well as how to manage the knowledge generated during the project life cycle. Basic project management tenets inform the practical steps to managing your design project. Management strategies also include techniques to gather and provide access to the 'knowledge' and expertise accrued during the project. It should be clear now that successful design projects require careful planning and expert coordination of the people and other resources (money, time, durable goods, etc.). The goal of these management efforts is not only to complete the task at hand, but also to inform project team members and stakeholders through the completion of the project. Theoretically, management implies that someone has been given (or has taken) the varied roles for a group of coordinating, communicating, facilitating, directing, mentoring, and monitoring. Members of the project team will bring unique knowledge, expertise, and experience to the endeavor. Furthermore, knowledge, expertise, and experience will accumulate during the lifetime of the project, requiring the management of these valuable resources. No doubt you probably have already observed that the techniques to create scenarios for information design outlined thus far will generate a tremendous amount of data for the project design team's use.

The authors have also outlined strategies for project management with an emphasis on the importance of the cycle of planning and evaluation that must occur to guide each step of the project. Such plans include not only a vision for the project but also the project goals and objectives as well as strategies and tactics to reach the predetermined project goals. Also critical to a project management plan is the application of evaluation criteria to assess the major areas of the planning process. The evaluation criteria include a consideration of the following:

- *Goal relatedness* – how does the activity fit into the overall goals for the organization?
- *Feasibility* – what is the potential for being successful?
- *Efficiency* – will this course of action provide optimum results rather than another course of action?
- *Effectiveness or impact.*

Keeping the project aligned to the project goals is ultimately the role of the project manager, but clearly defined and articulated goals will also guide the work of each member of the project team.

While acknowledging the difficulty of capturing a universally agreed upon definition of knowledge management, the authors have introduced a range of definitions of knowledge management from both the academic and popular literature. We finally agreed that for the purposes of this book, knowledge management is defined as not only the 'problem of capturing, organizing, and retrieving information, but is an activity that is inextricably bound up with human cognition in a human context' (Thomas, Kellogg and Erickson, 2001: 863). Information design demands embracing and understanding the complexities of human information seeking, information use in organizations, and organizational behaviour. For this reason, during the process of gathering data through the creation of information use scenarios information designers collect and assimilate data about the potential users of the systems under development, as well as gain expertise and insight. All of this data collection, analysis, and expertise building contributes to a body of 'knowledge' that not only is unique but also might be useful to all on the project team. Members of the information design team, therefore, use with regularity previously agreed upon tools to collect and manage the data gathered for a design project.

Moving on from the definitions, principles, and tools of project and knowledge management, the readers' attention was then focused on the methods for creating a 'knowledge community.'

A knowledge community requires building an infrastructure to communicate and present ideas among the project stakeholders. Because most large-scale information design projects have both internal and external stakeholders, all of whom may work in different technology environments with varied tools, the authors presented and explained various examples and methods for collecting and sharing data as well as how to ensure data quality. Guidelines and specific questions were proposed as a technique to establish an effective presentation and communications system. These questions included the following:

- Why do we need this particular presentation or communication system?

- What do we hope to gain from the system?
- How do we get what we want from the system?
- What can we do with the information we get from the system?

As a reminder, the team must use technologies for such a system that are the most appropriate for the stakeholders' skills and knowledge.

In Chapter 7 the authors encouraged the information design team to plan for the 'life cycle of ideas' within this knowledge community once a 'knowledge community' has been researched and developed. The line that separates knowledge management from 'managing' the life cycle of ideas is a fine one. This line of distinction, however, is infrequently discussed in the knowledge management literature. The life cycle of ideas requires attending to the components included in a knowledge management system. Such components include ideas, knowledge, documents, and assets. As a reminder, to manage knowledge requires identifying how stakeholders contribute and present ideas, as well as the modification and 'versioning' of these ideas.

Important to the life cycle of ideas is the point at which ideas become assets of the project, a concept fostered by the broadcasting, media, and publishing industries. Asset management requires long-term goals to serve a threefold purpose: the protection of intellectual properties, revenue generation, and the development of future ideas. Companies depend upon good idea management to learn about their success and failure, including: on-time delivery, productivity, employee turnover, cost-savings, and revenue generation. The life cycle of ideas involves three stages in a project for an information system: pre-project preparation, during project development, and post-project management. Ideas, knowledge, documents, and assets are critical ingredients for a successful implementation of the system project. They are not isolated from each other and represent information at different stages of an information system project. These key terms in a life cycle and their relationships with one another need to be identified for system design and development. From here the project team moves to the process of documentation of the project and prototyping the information system.

Chapter 8 directs the reader's attention to approaches and methods of documentation and prototyping for system development. Documentation includes recording and 'translating' the results of the stakeholder studies into notions for system prototyping and implementation. Based on the descriptions of user interaction scenarios, the system design team develops what Rosson and Carroll describe as 'conceptual-core models' (2001: 43). From these conceptual-core models the team begins to set standards for their prototypes and documentation developed from the user scenarios. Such documentation will evolve into system use documentation.

Conclusion

By now the reader has been introduced to a wide range of practical and theoretical tools to guide the information design process from the creation of life-like information-use scenarios to the application of ethnographic methods to better understand the client organization and its users. Techniques were explored for presenting and managing project ideas, processes, and knowledge, as well as documenting and prototyping the project. The information design process must accommodate the needs of information users as well as facilitate their interactions with information and information systems. Digital information design demands that designers cultivate both an open perspective and develop new skills to create information spaces that have imaginative and varied uses by diverse constituencies. The authors encourage the readers of this book to be vigilant and persuasive advocates on behalf of the users of information systems.

References

Rosson, M.B. and Carroll, J.M. (2001) 'Scenarios, objects, and points of view in user interface design,' in M. van Harmelen (ed.), *Object Modeling and User Interface Design*. Boston, MA: Addison-Wesley, pp. 36–69.

Thomas, J.C., Kellogg, W.A., and Erickson, T. (2001) 'The knowledge management puzzle: human and social factors in knowledge management,' *IBM Systems Journal*, 40 (4): 863–84.

Appendix:
Use of scenarios in information design – a checklist

1. Framework and fundamentals

(a) Determine the purpose of the system:

- internal system?
- external system?

(b) Begin the design plan by:

- defining necessary project steps
- establishing process workflows
- identifying targeted users
- distinguishing system users' activities
- instituting communication channels with users and design team
- implementing a useful, reliable system.

(c) Constitute a design team.

(d) Identify user group and environments:

- conduct user surveys
- identify variables
- identify human activities using system
- consider training and education.

2. **Organizational cultures: ecological and cognitive approaches**

   (a) Define and 'read' the client organization.

   - Locate an organization chart.

   - Interview individuals from 'all levels' of the organization to discuss the organizational hierarchy.

   - Ask respondents to identify seats of power and sources of information, both formal and informal.

   - Request a copy of an annual report or other documentation discussing the work of the organization.

   - Collect other 'artifacts' of the organization (T-shirts, brochures, pens, examples of employee awards, etc.).

   (b) Explore the organization using ethnographic research tools:

   - observation

   - interviews with members of the client organization

   - focus groups

   - case studies.

3. **Communicating with stakeholders**

   (a) Know who should be involved:

   - advisory committee

   - management committee.

   (b) Keeping them informed:

   - e-mail

   - mailing lists

   - online forums

   - information packets.

(c) Provide space for interaction:

- meetings
- teleconferencing
- on-site visits.

(d) Secure plans and ideas:

- content management
- track progress
- project management.

4. **Managing scenario design projects and knowledge**

(a) Determine who and what will be managed.

(b) Strategic planning and goal setting.

(c) Project management principles:

- establish project goals
- evaluate and select project goals:
  - goal relatedness
  - feasibility
  - efficiency
  - effectiveness or impact.

(d) Manage project knowledge:

- implement a network accessible database to store project data
- establish and agree upon group communication systems
- develop an online forum that interfaces with a searchable database to collect expertise and contact information
- establish a standard for subject fields and descriptors.

5. Presentation of ideas

(a) Establish a knowledge community:

- identify types of stakeholders:
  - internal
  - external.

(b) Plan for data management:

- sharable data
- data quality
- physical data
- digital data.

(c) Determine technologies appropriate for stakeholders and design team:

- hi tech or lo tech?
- dynamic data display
- data analysis
- multimedia.

6. Life cycle of ideas

(a) Determine the types of ideas:

- ideas and knowledge
- ideas and documents
- ideas and assets.

(b) Rationale for idea management:

- internal training
- evaluation of idea management:
  - on-time delivery
  - productivity
  - employee turnover
  - cost-savings

- challenges to idea management:
  - business competition
  - client turnover
  - quality control
  - post-project management.

7. Documentation and prototyping

(a) Setting prototype standards.

(b) Documentation of stakeholder studies and system development.

(c) Approaches to prototyping in system design:

- paper
- task analysis
- storyboards
- walk through method to test structure.

Complete references

Ackerman, M.S. (2002) 'The intellectual challenge of CSCW: the gap between social requirements and technical feasibility,' in J.M. Carroll (ed.), *Human–Computer Interaction in the New Millenium*. New York: ACM Press, pp. 303–24.

Ackerman, M.S., Pipek, V., and Wulf, V. (eds) (2003) *Sharing Expertise: Beyond Knowledge Management*. Cambridge, MA: MIT Press.

Arenson, K.W. (2003) 'Columbia's Internet concern will soon go out of business,' *New York Times*, January 7.

Arias, E., Eden, H., Fischer, G., Gorman, A., and Scharff, E. (2002) 'Transcending the individual human mind: creating shared understanding through collaborative design,' in J.M. Carroll (ed.), *Human–Computer Interaction in the New Millenium*. New York: ACM Press, pp. 347–72.

Artim, J.M. (2001) 'Entity, task, and presenter classification in user interface architecture,' in M. van Harmelen (ed.), *Object Modeling and User Interface Design*. Boston, MA: Addison-Wesley, pp. 115–58.

Berkman, E. (2001) 'When bad things happen to good ideas,' *Darwinmag.com*, April. Retrieved February 17, 2004, from: *http://www.darwinmag.com/read/040101/badthingss.html*.

Bryan-Kinns, N. and Hamilton, F. (2002) 'One for all and all for one? Case studies of using prototypes in commercial projects,' *NordiCHI*, October 19–23: 91–100.

Byrne, T. (2001) 'CM vs DM vs KM vs DAM vs SCM vs DRM – which one is right for you.' Retrieved January 7,

2005, from: *http://www.cmswatch.com/Features/ OpinionWatch/FeaturedOpinion/?feature_id=53*.

Carroll, J.M. (2000) *Making Use: Scenario-Based Design of Human–Computer Interactions*. Cambridge, MA: MIT Press.

Choo, C.W. (1998) *The Knowing Organization: How Organizations Use Information to Construct Meaning, Create Knowledge, and Make Decisions*. Oxford: Oxford University Press.

Cool, C. and Spink, A. (2002) 'Issues of context in information retrieval (IR): an introduction to the special issue,' *Information Processing and Management*, 38 (5): 605–11.

Dennis, A. and Wixom, B.H. (2000) *Systems Analysis and Design*. New York: John Wiley & Sons.

Denzin, N. and Lincoln, Y.S. (2002) *Handbook of Qualitative Research*, 2nd edn. Thousand Oaks: CA: Sage.

Ergazakis, K. et al. (2002) 'Knowledge management in enterprises: a research agenda,' in D. Karagiannis and U. Reimer (eds), *Practical Aspects of Knowledge Management*. Berlin: Springer, pp. 37–58.

Erickson, T. (1995) 'Notes on design practice: stories and prototypes as catalysts,' in J.M. Carroll (ed.), *Scenario-Based Design: Envisioning Work and Technology in System Development*. New York: John Wiley & Sons, pp. 37–58.

Erickson, T. and Kellogg, W.A. (2002) 'Social translucence: designing systems that support social process,' in J.M. Carroll (ed.), *Human–Computer Interaction in the New Millennium*. New York: ACM Press, pp. 325–45.

Glesne, C. (1999) *Becoming Qualitative Researchers: An Introduction*, 2nd edn. New York: Longman.

Gorman, G.E. and Clayton, P. (eds) (1997) *Qualitative Research for the Information Professional*. London: Library Association Publishing.

Hannaford, S. and Poyssick, G. (1999) *Teams and the Graphics Arts Service Provider*. Upper Saddle River, NJ: Prentice Hall PTR.

Hill, G.M. (2004) *The Complete Project Management Office Handbook*. New York: Auerbauch.

International Organization for Standardization (ISO) (2005a) 'ISO 9000 and ISO 14000 – in brief.' Retrieved February 20, 2005, from: *http://www.iso.org/iso/en/ iso9000-14000/index.html*.

International Organization for Standardization (ISO) (2005b) 'Quality management principles.' Retrieved February 20, 2005, from: *http://www.iso.org/iso/en/ iso9000-14000/iso9000/qmp.html*.

Kjellin, H. and Stenfors, T. (2002) 'Process for acquiring knowledge while sharing knowledge,' in D. Karagiannis and U. Reimer (eds), *Practical Aspects of Knowledge Management*. Berlin: Springer, pp. 268–80.

Kliem, R. and Ludin, I.S. (1998) *Project Management Practitioner's Handbook*. New York: AMACOM.

Knight, T. and Howes, T. (2003) *Knowledge Management – A Blueprint for Delivery: A Programme for Mobilizing Knowledge and Building the Learning Organization*. Oxford: Butterworth Heinemann.

Koenig, M.E.D. (1999) 'Education for knowledge management,' *Information Services and Users*, 19: 17–31.

Krueger, R.A. and Casey, M.A. (2000) *Focus Groups: A Practical Guide for Applied Research*. Thousand Oaks, CA: Sage.

Levy, D.M. (2003) 'Documents and libraries: a sociotechnical perspective,' in A.P. Bishop, N.A. Van House, and B.P. Buttenfield (eds), *Digital Library Use: Social Practice in Design and Evaluation*. Cambridge, MA: MIT Press, pp. 25–42.

Nardi, A.B. (1995) 'Some reflections on scenarios,' in J.M. Carroll (ed.), *Scenario-Based Design: Envisioning Work and Technology in System Development.* New York: John Wiley & Sons, pp. 387–99.

Norman, D.A. (1993) *Things That Make Us Smart.* Reading, MA: Addison-Wesley.

Northwest Airlines. Retrieved September 19, 2005, from: *http://nwa.com.*

Object by Design. 'Choosing a UML Modeling Tool.' Retrieved September 19, 2005, from: *http://www .objectsbydesign.com/tools/modeling_tools.html.*

Object Management Group (OMG). 'Introduction to OMG's Unified Modeling Language™ (UML®).' Retrieved September 19, 2005, from: *http://www.omg.org/ gettingstarted/what_is_uml.htm.*

Object Management Group (OMG). 'Introduction to OMG's Unified Modeling Language™ (UML®).' Retrieved November 2, 2005, from: *http://www.omg.org/ gettingstarted/what_is_uml.htm.*

Olsen, F. (2002). 'Software-coding costs force Indiana U. at Bloomington to drop a popular graduation guarantee,' *Chronicle of Higher Education.* Available at: *http:// chronicle.com/free/2002/12/2002120501t.htm.*

Oxford English Dictionary (OED Online) (1989) 2nd edn. Retrieved September 19, 2005.

Patton, M. (1990) *Qualitative Evaluation and Research Methods,* 2nd edn. Newbury Park, CA: Sage.

Rice-Lively, M. (1997) 'Sensemaking in the electronic reference centre: an ethnographic study,' in G.E. Gorman and P. Clayton (eds), *Qualitative Research for the Information Professional.* London: Library Association Publishing.

Rosenfeld, L. and Morville, P. (1998) *Information Architecture for the World Wide Web.* Cambridge, UK and Sebastopol, CA: O'Reilly.

Rosson, M.B. and Carroll, J.M. (2001) 'Scenarios, objects, and points of view in user interface design,' in M. van Harmelen (ed.), *Object Modeling and User Interface Design*. Boston, MA: Addison-Wesley, pp. 39–69.

Schonlau, M., Fricker, R.D., and Elliott, M.N. (2002) *Conducting Research Surveys via E-Mail and the Web*. Santa Monica, CA: Rand.

Section 508. Retrieved September 19, 2005, from *http://www.section508.gov*.

Snyder, C. (2003) *Paper Prototyping: The Fast and Easy Way to Design and Refine User Interfaces*. Amsterdam: Morgan Kaufmann.

Starbuck, W.H. and Milliken, F.J. (1988) 'Executives' perceptual filters: What they notice and how they make sense,' in D.C. Hambrick (ed.), *The Executive Effect: Concepts and Methods for Studying Top Managers*. Greenwich, CT: JAI Press, pp. 35–65.

Thomas, J.C., Kellogg, W., and Erickson, T. (2001) 'The knowledge management puzzle: human and social factors in knowledge management,' *IBM Systems Journal*, 40 (4): 863–84.

US Census Bureau. 'Annual Estimates of the Population for Counties of Alabama.' Retrieved March 15, 2005, from: *http://www.census.gov/popest/counties/tables/CO-EST2003-01-01.pdf*.

US Census Bureau. 'Distribution of Population by County Population Size.' Retrieved March 15, 2005, from: *http://www.census.gov/popest/gallery/graphs/CO-distpop.html*.

US Census Bureau. 'Population Size for Counties.' Retrieved March 15, 2005, from: *http://www.census.gov/popest/gallery/maps/popsize_c3.html*.

Wiki. 'Wikipedia: The free encyclopedia.' Retrieved August 21, 2005, from: *http://www.wikipedia.org*.

Wirfs-Brock, R. and McKean, A. (2003) *Object Design: Roles, Responsibilities, and Collaborations.* Boston, MA: Addison-Wesley.

Index

Printed in the United States
50723LVS00002B/119